MW01102467

The
IMMIGRATION
Handbook

For Work, Investment, Study
and Retirement
in the U.S.A.

Henry G. Liebman

Cover and book design: Chris Davis
Copy Editor: Jeff Shelley
Layout: Anni Shelley

Published by Fairgreens Media, Inc.
Fairgreens Media, Inc.
P.O. Box 15330
Seattle, WA 98115-0330
(206) 525-1294

Library of Congress Cataloging-in-Publication Data
Liebman, Henry G., 1951-
The Immigration Handbook/Henry G. Liebman
p.   cm.
Includes index.
ISBN 0-9629329-1-4

Library of Congress Catalog Card Number 95-83466

Printed in the U.S.A.

$8.95 U.S., $11.95 Canadian

This book is dedicated to my staff
and colleagues who have made my
professional success possible.

Table of Contents

Preface   1

1. The History of U.S. Immigration   3

The First Attempts at Limiting Immigrants   4
The Modern Immigration System   5
New Steps to Curtail 'Illegals'   5
A Trend Toward More Restrictions   6
What the Future Bodes   7

2. Background & Basics of Visas   9

What Is a Visa?   10
Two Categories of Visas   10
    Nonimmigrant Visas   10
    Immigrant Visas   10
    Who Processes Visas?   11
    INS Preapproval   12
    Consular Processing   12
How the INS & Consuls Evaluate Visa Petitions:
    The Process   12
Upon Receiving a Visa Application for Entry to the U.S.:
    Green Light to Enter   13
Form I-94 & Visa Expiration Dates   13
Denial of Entry & Your Options   13
Change of Status & Extension of Stays   14
Visa Revalidation   15
Honesty is Best Policy . . .and Best Way to Obtain a Visa   15
Recapping This Chapter   16

3. The B-1 Visa — Business Visitors   19

Who's Eligible for B-1 Visas?   20
What Constitutes Work?   21

Application Procedures & Strategy   22
B-1 versus Visa Waiver   23
B-1 Advantages   23
Use B-1 Visas Only In Special Cases   24

4. The B-2 Visa — How to Travel for Pleasure   **25**
Problems with Single Young Adults, Parents & Students   26
Students   26
Young Adults   27

5. Temporary Working Visas   **29**
General   30
Terminology   31
    Professionals   31
    Executive/Manager   31
    International Organization   31
    Essential Skill & Specialized Knowledge 31
L Visas: Intra-Company Transference   32
    Branch Office in the U.S.   33
    Subsidiary Company   33
    Affiliated Company   33
Treaty Trader/Investor—Basic Terminology   33
    E Visa Processing   34
    The Treaties   35
Control & Ownership of a U.S. Treaty Company   36
Treaty Trader: E-1 Visa   36
    Direct Trade   37
    Trade Primarily Between the U.S. & a Treaty Country 37
Treaty Investor E-2   38
Basic Requirements of H Visas: For Professional Workers   39
    H-1B Employer   39
    The Labor Conditions Application Process 40

Professional Licenses   41

When to Use H, L or E   42

Summary of Eligibility for E, H & L Visa Holders   43

6. Staffing for a New Business in America   45

Establish the U.S. Company First   46

Have a Premise for Doing Business   46

The Visa Application   47

A Case Study   47

Alternatives to the L-1A Approach: E-2 & H-1B   48

After a One-Year Period   49

Dependent Children   51

7. Staffing an Existing U.S. Business   53

Choosing the Correct Visa   54

Managers   54

    Factors Favoring E Visas   55

    Factors Favoring H & L Visas   56

H-1B Visas   57

Common Applications of H-1 Visas   58

    Financial & Business Professionals   58

Engineers   59

Summary   60

Specialized Knowledge & Essential Skills   61

    Who Can Use L-1B & E Essential Skill Visas   63

    The "Technicians" Option   64

Recruitment Difficulties   65

Other H-2B Applications   65

    Marine Products Technicians   66

Review of Guidelines for Specialists   67

Rectifying the "Foreign" Image   67

Wage & Promotional Discrimination   68

8. Five Ways to Obtain a "Green Card"   71

General Concepts   72
The Petition   73
The Quota   73
Green Card Interview   74
Exclusion   76
Green Card Categories   76
Pursue the Easiest Method First - Family Class   76
The Petition   77
Planning for the Quota Waiting Period   77
Negotiating the Waiting Period with a B-2 Visa   78
Negotiating the Quota Waiting Period by Finding a Job   79
Negotiating the Quota Waiting Period As a Student   80
In Sum   80
For the Wealthy - An "Investor Program"   80
Employee Criteria   81
Investment Fund Sources   82
Business Plan   82
The "Regional Center" Program   82
Some Pitfalls with Regional Center Investments   83
Who Manages Regional Centers?   84
Retirement in America - "The Two-Step" Method For Managers & Executives   85
A Common Scenario   86
The First Step   86
The Second Step   86
Details of the Two-Step Process   87
Step 1. Establish the U.S. Business/Managerial Transfer with a Nonimmigrant Work Visa   87
Establishing a U.S. Subsidiary   87
Choosing a Nonimmigrant Work Visa   88

Step 2. One Year of Doing Business, Multinational
Manager Green Card   89

Another Two-Step Approach:
Green Cards for Corporate Executives or Managers
& Established Organizations   90

   Benefits for Children & Retirement   90

   Employer's Point of View   91

  Timing & Procedure   92

   Nonimmigrant Work Visa (Step 1)   92

   Green Card (Step 2)   92

  The Green Card Interview   92

   INS Interview   92

   Consular Interview   93

The Green Card   93

   Separate Interviews for Family Members   93

  Travel During the INS Interview Process   94

  Common Pitfalls   95

  Conclusion   96

  Those with Extraordinary Abilities in Sciences,
Arts & Business   96

National Interest   96

The Last Resort: Labor Certification   98

  General   98

  Job Requirements & Prevailing Wage   99

  Labor Certification Forms   100

  Steps in the Labor Certification Process   100

  Step 1. Creating the Job Description   100

  Sample Job Description—Block 12   101

Strategy   101

  Education & Experience—Block 13   102

   Strategy   102

A Trap: Experience Gained with the Petitioning
    Employer   103
Special Requirements—Block 14   103
Strategy   104
Step 2: State Job Service Processing   104
Step 3: Recruitment   105
Step 4: Department of Labor Approval   106
Step 5: INS Approval   107
Keeping Your Green Card   107
    Reentry Permits   108
Tax Returns   109
Permits to Re-enter   110
Green Card   110
When Tax & Immigration Laws Conflict   111
An Example of Green Card Forfeiture   111
Summary   113

9. Student Visas   **115**

General Procedures   116
    Travel on a Student Visa   117
    Financial Support   117
Strict Enforcement   117
Where to Get Assistance   118
Three Key Questions Need The Same Answer: Yes   118
Working While Studying   119
    On-Campus Employment   119
    Pilot Off-Campus Employment Program   119
    Curricular Practical Training   119
Post-Completion Practical Training Program   120
Options After Practical Training   120

10. Visas for the Privileged, Media, Athletes, Entertainers,Cultural Exchanges, Religious Workers & Tycoons   123

I Visa for Information Media   124

O Visa for Oustanding Actors, Businesspeople & Artists   124

P Visa for Sports Teams, Athletes
    & Entertainment Groups   126

Q Visa for Cultural Exchange Programs   126

R Visa Religious Workers   126

    Ministers   127

    Religious Workers   128

Details About NAFTA   129

    Expedited Procedures for Canadians under NAFTA   129

    Strategy   130

11. Naturalization - Becoming An American Citizen   131

Advantages of Citizenship   132

Dual Citizenship   133

The Qualifying Period   133

The Citizenship Test   134

Certificate of Naturalization   135

Appendices   137

A. Glossary   138

B. Immigration Forms & Other Documents   142

    Forms Requiring No Filing Fees   142

    Forms Requiring Fees   142

C. Visa Categories   147

    Nonimmigrant Visa Categories   147

    Permanent Resident Visa Categories   149

        Family-Sponsored Preferences   149

        Employment-Based Preferences   149

D. Important Addresses   150

    Immigration & Naturalization Service Centers   150

    Consulates   152

    Visa Office   152

E. Suggested Document Lists   153

    E-1 Treaty Trader Visa Application   153

    E-2 Treaty Investor Visa Application   154

    H-1 Professional Visa Application   155

    L-1 (Intracompany Transferees in an Executive,
       Managerial or Specialized Knowledge Capacity)
      Visa Application   156

F. Proposed Changes in U.S. Immigration Law

    Permanent Residence Employment-Based
    Visa Categories   158

    Labor Certification   158

    L-1A   158

    H-1B   158

    E-2 Eligibility   159

    Family Class Green Card   159

    Investor Category   159

    Other Possible Changes   159

    Author's Predictions   160

About the Author   161

Legal Assistance   161

Preface

The United States and Canada accept more immigrants today than since the early 1900s. Several million tourists, temporary workers, asylees, refugees and permanent residents come to North America each year. America's "melting pot" and Canada's "mosaic," once almost entirely European, now includes people from every corner of the planet. People move to North America for freedom, safety and opportunity, while appreciating the unique blend of living space, political stability and high standard of living.

North America is relatively open to immigrants. However, as the continent fills with new arrivals, the doors will slowly close. During the first 150 years of its history, the U.S. accepted whoever arrived. Since the 1920s, American immigration laws have regulated and prioritized the flow of immigrants. Immigrating to the U.S. now requires foreigners seeking entry to position themselves in the most advantageous immigrant categories.

Possible New Legislation

One of the hallmarks of immigration law is its constant state of flux. We've tried our best to give readers the most up-to-date information, but sometimes it's difficult to foresee how the laws will ultimately read. In an effort to help convey the latest trends in immigration law, notes have been placed in appropriate places throughout the book to describe possible changes to particular laws.

Simplifying a Complex Subject

After practicing immigration law for 15 years, I've found that most clients pose the same questions. Businessmen needing to bring critical personnel to the U.S. typically ask: "How do I get my workers into the U.S.? How long does it take? And how much will it cost?" Almost everyone wants to know, "How do I get a green card?"

Mere regurgitation of U.S. immigration laws confuses clients. Most people want to know the steps required to immigrate, their options, how long the process takes, and their chances for success. They want the information presented in a simple, logical way. This book simplifies the complex subject in a way which I hope you'll find understandable and accessible.

It discusses immigration strategies for most scenarios. There are many confusing paths leading to a green card—the nonimmigrant visa list starts at "A" and ends at "S." The list includes diplomats, vessel crew members, U.N. officials, NATO generals and staff, religious workers, as well as the more commonly used working visas. This book concisely points out the obstacles often encountered with an immigration scenario, and provides solutions.

- It explains how to obtain the best visa for your purposes—for work, investment, study in universities, or permanent residence.

- It teaches you how to interact with Immigration and Naturalization Service (INS) inspectors at border crossings and airports.

- It provides pointers for effective communication with consular officers when applying for visas abroad.

After reading this book you'll be able to choose the best immigration strategy to accomplish your ultimate goal. You may even feel confident enough to handle your own case. At a minimum, you'll be able to tell your lawyer what you hope to accomplish.

Chapter 1

The History of U.S. Immigration

For all practical purposes, the U.S. had open borders until 1875. Many states actually promoted immigration as the U.S. needed settlers to tame the North American wilderness, and most of the new arrivals came from Northern Europe.

The first serious attempts to limit immigration occurred through a series of laws enacted between 1875 and 1917. These laws excluded lunatics, convicts, all Chinese peoples, beggars, anarchists, and carriers of contagious diseases. Immigrants during this period were assessed a 50-cents-per-person tax.

At the onset of the 20th Century, the U.S. received upwards of one million immigrants per year. Most of the new arrivals came from Eastern and Southern Europe, and tended to be Roman Catholic, Eastern Orthodox or Jewish, as opposed to America's predominant religion at that time, Protestant Christianity. Many newcomers couldn't read or speak English.

The First Attempts at Limiting Immigrants

A series of laws enacted between 1917 and 1924 attempted to limit the number of new immigrants. These laws expanded the categories of excludable aliens, established the quota system, and banned all Asians except Japanese, who had made a "Gentleman's Agreement" with the U.S.

The quota system restricted the number of visas made available to particular nationalities. The system, which allocated visas according to the number of persons of the same nationality living in the U.S., favored the majority ethnic groups, namely the Northern Europeans. The quota system limited the total visas issued to 150,000 per year, with no restrictions on persons born in the Western Hemisphere. Additionally, the U.S. Congress decided to bar citizenship to "Orientals," which meant that Asians, including Japanese, could no longer become U.S. citizens.

By 1924, U.S. immigration law limited the total number of aliens and imposed qualitative restrictions.

The Modern Immigration System

The next major change in immigration law occurred with the 1952 Act, which established the modern immigration system. The new quota system created limits on a per-country basis without regard to the number of persons of particular nationalities currently living in the U.S. Asian immigration was limited, rather than restricted.

The 1952 Act also established the preference system that gave priority to family members and people with special skills. This was the first attempt to target immigrants with special skills.

Subsequent changes to the immigration laws were driven by a more enlightened attitude toward civil rights. Positive changes were also due to the increasing need for U.S. multinational corporations to attract skilled labor, and to transfer key personnel between the U.S. and foreign operations.

In 1968 Congress officially abolished restrictions on Oriental immigration. It also eliminated immigration discrimination based on race, place of birth, sex and residence. In 1970 Congress implemented the L-1—or managerial-transfer—program. In 1976 Congress eliminated preferential treatment for residents of the Western Hemisphere.

New Steps to Curtail 'Illegals'

By 1986 the U.S. was facing the biggest immigration wave since the turn of the century. Only this time the majority of immigrants were from Latin America and Asia. The West Coast of the U.S. and the border states with Mexico and Cuba received the brunt of these new arrivals.

By some estimates, the number of 'illegals' exceeded the number of legal immigrants.

In 1986 changes to the immigration laws were intended to tighten up the system. Congress legalized hundreds of thousands of illegal immigrants, while introducing the employer-sanctions program which fines employers for hiring illegal workers. To curtail an epidemic of bogus marriages to U.S. citizens, Congress passed tough laws to prevent marriage fraud.

While the 1986 Act focused on curtailing illegal immigration, the 1990 Act was aimed at helping U.S. businesses attract skilled foreign workers. The 1990 Act established an annual limit of 675,000 permanent resident visas; 465,000 for family class; 140,000 for employment-based categories; and 55,000 for the visa lottery. On top of these limits, the law permits 125,000 refugees and smaller groups authorized by prior laws.

The 1990 Act also increased the number of employment-based visas from approximately 54,000 annually to 140,000 a year. The expanded business-class categories favor persons who make educational, professional, or financial contributions. For example, the 1990 Act created the Immigrant Investor Program. Conversely, the 1990 Act limited the number of non-immigrant visas available to professional workers to 65,000 per year. So far, none of the quota or numerical limitations of the 1990 Act for non-immigrant visas have been reached.

A Trend Toward More Restrictions

Today, the national debate has shifted to restricting immigration. Almost every national magazine and newspaper has run feature articles implying that immigrants take jobs from Americans. There are serious discussions on the negative effects immigration has on social services. The state of California recently passed a law that denies welfare benefits to illegals. Many politicians believe America needs a "rest" from immigration, saying time is needed to absorb the millions of immigrants recently allowed into the country. Still other politicians want to liberalize employment- and investor-based immigration.

The U.S. Congress has been considering legislation that may restrict family-class and employment-based categories while increasing experience requirements for professional workers.

What the Future Bodes

Congress will try to balance the number of newcomers the country can absorb with the rights of families to re-unify, the needs of businesses to attract the best workers in the world, and the need to attract foreign capital. The late-1990s will see repeated attempts to "tighten up the system" and lessen the impact on American social services. On the other hand, the weak dollar and growing internationalism of U.S. business will work to maintain or increase current levels of employment-based immigration.

Overall, we can expect continued pressure to reduce the numbers of immigrants, while at the same time improving the quality of their skills. I expect to see family-class categories limited to immediate family members, and higher educational and/or experience requirements for professional workers. There may be more encouragement for foreign investors.

The beauty of American immigration law is that the U.S. has moved from an ethnically-biased system which favored Northern Europeans to one that is truly multinational and allows freedom and opportunity for all. The U.S. offers the only immigration policy in the world that is blind to race, religion, creed and color. It's truly a unique social experiment that continues to evolve.

Chapter 2

Background & Basics of Visas

This chapter explains the visa issuance procedure, applications for entry to the U.S. at airports and land border crossings, changes of status from one visa category to another, and extensions of visas.

What Is a Visa?

A visa—usually stamped in a passport—permits the bearer to apply for entry into a country. The U.S. requires visas, unless a country qualifies for a visa waiver. Most European countries and Japan qualify for visa waivers. A visa waiver eliminates the visa requirement for business and pleasure trips under 90 days in duration. Those who plan to work in the U.S. need a visa regardless of how long they intend to remain in the country. Foreigners living in the U.S. for indefinite periods need a "green card," or a visa for permanent resident status.

Two Categories of Visas

Visas are either nonimmigrant, i.e. temporary, or immigrant, permanent. Refer to the Glossary for definitions of the various visa categories and the appropriate chapters for full details.

Nonimmigrant Visas

The holder of a nonimmigrant visa agrees to leave the U.S. prior to the end of a permitted stay period. The U.S. issues over 30 types of nonimmigrant visas designated by letters of the alphabet. The nonimmigrant visa holder may only engage in the designated activity or work for a designated employer. Validity periods vary with the type of nonimmigrant visa.

Immigrant Visas

An immigrant visa permits the holder to live in the U.S. for as long as the U.S. is the permanent place of residence. Immigrant visa holders may engage in any activity and work for any employer without restrictions. The INS issues immigrant visa holders an Alien Registration Card to evidence permanent resident status. The card, now pinkish-blue, was once green in color, hence its name, the "green card."

Green card holders enjoy all the rights and obligations of U.S. citizens except that they cannot vote. Green card holders may apply for citizenship after the passage of three years for spouses of U.S. citizens, or five years for all other green card holders. Green card holders must file U.S. income tax returns and, in the case of war, serve in the U.S. armed forces if called to duty.

Who Processes Visas?

Overseas, foreign service officers and U.S. consular posts issue all visas; you must obtain your first visa from a consular officer outside the U.S. These consuls work for the Department of State, an agency of the federal government that controls the country's foreign affairs. Each U.S. consular post determines its own filing procedure, and not all consular posts process visas. Ask the consular post nearest your home for its procedures before applying.

Most visa categories require INS approval before application at the consulate for a visa stamp. The INS, which is part of the Department of Justice, approves visa petitions but cannot issue visas.

Not every visa category requires INS preapproval. Exceptions include:

- B-1/B-2 Temporary Business or Tourist Visas
- E-1/2 Treaty Trader and Treaty Investor
- I Information Media
- R Religious Workers
- And select categories pertaining to diplomats, military personnel, and special cases.

INS Preapproval

In order to obtain INS visa approval, file your petition and supporting documents by mail or courier with one of the U.S. Regional Processing Centers in Vermont, Texas, California or Nebraska (see the Appendices for addresses). Upon receipt and review of your filing, the INS will mail you its decision. If the INS approves your petition, take the approval notice (Form I-797), Consular Visa Application (Form OF-156), and your passport to the U.S. consulate in your area and apply for the visa.

Consular Processing

Consuls decide who receives a visa. The consul may accept an INS preapproval, or the officer may ask you for more information, conduct an interview, or deny your visa application. The consul may deny your visa application even though the INS approved the petition. Normally the consul will issue the visa petition if the INS approves it. Upon approval the consul places the visa stamp in your passport. The stamp shows the place and date of issue, the number of permitted entries, duration, visa type, and if applicable, the name of the U.S. employer.

How the INS & Consuls Evaluate Visa Petitions: The Process

The INS adjudicates visa petitions solely upon the information contained in the forms, the cover letter and supporting documents. The INS makes no personal contact with the applicant. The consulate bases its decision upon the same criteria, except that it may request a personal interview. As a rule, consulates request interviews only when they suspect a problem with a case. Both INS and consular applications require detailed documentation.

Upon Receiving a Visa Application for Entry to the U.S.: Green Light to Enter

Once a visa is obtained you may apply for entry into the U.S. The INS controls who enters the country, just as a consul controls who receives visas. The INS may deny your entry into the U.S. even though you may have a valid visa. If the INS admits you into the U.S. it will stamp your Arrival Departure Card (Form I-94) with the date of entry, visa type and expiration date. The I-94 card issued by the INS determines how long you may stay in the U.S. Airline flight attendants distribute I-94 forms before landing at an international airport.

Form I-94 & Visa Expiration Dates

The expiration dates on the I-94 card and your visa may differ. The I-94 form shows how long you may stay in the U.S., while the visa merely indicates the period during which you may apply for entry. For example, a multiple-entry visa, valid for three years, permits unlimited applications to enter the U.S. during the three-year period.

You must leave the U.S. or extend your I-94 by the I-94 expiration date even if your visa is valid beyond that period. For example, you have a three-year visa but the INS only admits you for two years. In other words, the I-94 form expires before the visa does. In this case you must leave the U.S., or extend your I-94 form prior to the I-94 expiration date—even though you have a valid visa.

Denial of Entry & Your Options

Denial of U.S. entry occurs when the INS suspects that your visa does not permit the purpose of your trip into the country. For example, a person presents a B-1 visa but the INS suspects that the person will work in the U.S. Or a spouse attempts entry on a tourist visa when, in fact, she intends to live in the U.S.

All visa holders have a right to a hearing so they may argue their case. One of the major drawbacks of requesting a hearing is that you may have to wait in jail for a few days prior to the trial date. For this reason most people return immediately to their country of origin. (Note that people entering the U.S. on visa waiver have no right to a hearing.) If the INS permits you to voluntarily return home, you may reapply for entry to the U.S. anytime. If you are deported at U.S. government expense, you must wait up to five years before being eligible to apply for re-entry to the U.S.

Change of Status & Extension of Stays

Once admitted to the U.S., a change in plans or employment may require an extension of stay or change in visa status. Provided that you did not violate the terms of your stay, you may extend the I-94 form or change immigration status while in the U.S. Applications for extensions or changes of status must be made through one of the INS Regional Processing Centers by filing appropriate forms and supporting documents. The INS must receive such petitions on or before the I-94 expiration date. Other than exceptional circumstances, the INS denies I-94 extension petitions that are filed late. You may remain in the U.S. during the process, even if the processing period extends beyond the I-94 validity date.

Extensions require proof that you intend to stay in the U.S. in the same employment capacity, and you must explain why you need the extension. The INS treats changes from one nonimmigrant status to another nonimmigrant status as a new petition. INS approval of an extension or change of status only permits you to remain in the U.S.; you need a valid visa if you leave and wish to re-enter the country.

Visa Revalidation

You may revalidate an expired visa while in the U.S. The Visa Office in Washington, D.C. only accepts mail-in applications for visa revalidation. In addition to the documentation required for any petition, applicants must prove that they have a valid I-94 card at the time of application. Those who don't qualify for revalidation must apply for their visa abroad.

The Visa Office provides a convenient alternative to traveling abroad for visa holders who qualify for revalidation, but it only revalidates the same visa category. For example, a person with an expired L-1A visa may apply for another L-1A visa through the Visa Office. A person changing from L-1A to E-1 may not apply for revalidation.

NOTE: Canadians do not need a visa to enter the U.S. They may skip the consular step and apply for entry at a border crossing. In most cases, Canadians obtain INS preapproval and present the approval notice to the INS inspector at the border. NAFTA permits Canadians to file petitions at certain border points. In any event, the INS issues form I-94 to evidence the correct status. As an example, a Canadian could take the L-1 approval notice directly to a border crossing to obtain an L-1 I-94, or apply for the L-1 at the border.

Honesty is the Best Policy . . . and the Best Way to Obtain a Visa

It's always best to tell the truth to consuls and INS immigration inspectors. When you tell the truth most inspectors and consuls will try to help solve your immigration problems. But if you lie to them no one will help. Worst of all, you can be barred from the U.S. for life if the inspector or consul believes that fraud was committed or facts were materially misrepresented during the visa application process.

Visa applicants often lie when the truth would have worked much better. Avoid overly preparing for the application process. Don't try to be an expert with visa applications, and don't try to anticipate what the inspector and consul want to hear. If you calmly tell the truth you'll encounter more helpful government officials and fewer problems at the international airport or port of entry. You will also save money on legal fees.

Recapping This Chapter

- A visa allows you to apply for admission to the U.S.

- Only U.S. consuls issue visas.

- A single-entry visa allows you to apply for entry one time within the visa validity period.

- A multiple-entry visa permits you to apply for entry unlimited times within the visa validity period.

- You apply for admission to the U.S. when your passport is shown to the INS inspector at the airport or port of entry.

- The INS determines who enters the U.S. and length of stay.

- The I-94 card issued by the INS indicates how long you may stay in the U.S.

- Once inside the U.S., if you maintain legal status, you may extend your stay or change to another immigration status.

- If you leave the U.S. you must have a valid visa to re-enter.

- Tell the truth to consuls and INS immigration inspectors and you'll be much better off.

Now let's discuss the specific visa categories.

Chapter 3

The B-1 Visa — Business Visitors

The B-1 visa allows visits to the U.S. for business trips of under six months in duration.

B-1 visa holders may not be employed by a U.S. company. Permissible business activities within the B-1 category may include:

- A series of business meetings
- Scientific collaboration
- Inspection of business opportunities
- Meetings with government officials
- Purchase of products
- Negotiating contracts to buy or sell products or services
- Selling of products
- Certain warranty and repair work.

B-1 visa holders must be paid from abroad. Their activities must also be directed from abroad, and they must plan to depart the U.S. within six months. Under visa waiver one may conduct the same activities, but only within 90 days.

Who's Eligible for B-1 Visas?

Businesspeople eligible for a B-1 visa include the following:

- Consulting engineers
- Scientists and professionals involved in joint projects with U.S. counterparts
- Salespeople
- Academicians collaborating with U.S. counterparts
- Marine products buyers
- Warranty and repair technicians coming to the U.S. per warranty and repair contracts

• Purchasing agents.

Specialized foreign-made equipment sold within the U.S. often comes with a warranty and repair agreement. Foreign technicians may make warranty and repair service calls using a B-1 visa within one year after the sale of a product, pursuant to a written contract between the buyer and seller promising the warranty and repair services. This is the only exception to the general rule prohibiting B-1 visa holders from working in the U.S.

To avoid problems at ports of entry, all B-1 visitors should carry documents that prove the purpose of their trip. Effective documentation may include:

• A copy of the warranty and repair contract

• An explanatory letter from the employer

• A letter of invitation from a U.S. business contact

• A detailed itinerary of meetings.

Also recommended is having someone knowledgeable meet you at the airport or point of entry, in case you need to explain the purpose of your trip or need language assistance.

What Constitutes Work?

The primary purpose of the Immigration and Nationality Act is to protect American workers, and B-1 business visitors may not work in the U.S. INS statistics reveal that many B-1 visitors work in the U.S. illegally instead of taking the time to obtain a proper work visa. This makes B-1 visa holders a suspect class. Additionally, B-1 visa holders do not pay U.S. income tax, while holders of most working visas pay income taxes.

Work means that your activity takes an American job.

On one hand, it is difficult to let a U.S. citizen handle your business meetings or represent you in professional collaborations. On the other hand, U.S. citizens can manufacture goods or perform professional services. B-1 visa holders must convince the consul and INS inspector that they intend to conduct business and not engage in employment.

INS inspectors suspect frequent B-1 visitors as well as those who handle equipment while working in the U.S. If your activity in the U.S. is connected with creating or manufacturing a product, or directing subordinate employees, expect problems. Legally, B-1 visitors may handle products or equipment "incidental" to purchase, sales or demonstration. B-1 holders may also visit branch offices or affiliated companies for a series of collaborations and meetings.

As a practical matter, it is difficult to convince an INS inspector that you alone are "incidentally" handling a product. It's also difficult for the frequent B-1 visitor coming to the same U.S. office to claim he or she doesn't direct employees or provide a service. Common sense dictates that the more time you spend in the U.S., the more involved you are in the creation of a product or provision of a service. Thus, the more likely you actually work in the U.S. In any event, since the INS suspects a frequent B-1 visa traveler of working in the U.S., that person faces more scrutiny than most other visa categories.

Application Procedures & Strategy

One must apply for a B-1 visa at a U.S. consulate. Provide the consular officer with background data to support the B-1 visa application. Important documentation includes:

- A detailed itinerary.

- Reasons for needing more than 90 days, if you are eligible for visa waiver, to conduct your business in the U.S.

- Proof that you will be paid from abroad.

- And proof that you're either an independent businessperson, or a foreign employer who controls your own U.S. activities.

Even if the consul approves a B-1 visa, you still must convince an INS inspector upon arrival in the U.S. that you qualify for the B-1 visa. As in all visa matters, it is a two-step process: first you must make your case to the consul, after which you make your case to the INS inspector. You must pass both tests in order to enter the U.S.

B-1 Versus Visa Waiver

From the INS inspector's point of view, the fact that you obtained a B-1 visa indicates that a consul reviewed the file. This makes your statements to the inspector more believable. If you enter on a visa waiver, the inspector knows that no one reviewed your file. The INS inspector also knows that with visa waiver he can send you home without a hearing. We recommend that business travelers apply for a B-1 visa and carefully document the purpose of their trip.

B-1 Advantages

People apply for B-1 visas for convenience and tax reasons. The B-1 visa is convenient in that you only make one application to the U.S. Consul, as opposed to applying first to the INS and then to the consul as in the case of most nonimmigrant work visas.

Since B-1 visa holders cannot work in the U.S. they do not pay American taxes. If you have a nonimmigrant work visa (E, H or L) and work in the U.S., you must pay taxes on American earnings. Meanwhile, B-1 visa holders may engage in some of the same activites and not pay U.S. taxes.

NOTE: The INS does not issue B-1 I-94s to Canadians. Canadians merely state the purpose of their business trip at a port of entry. If the reasons are satisfactory, the inspector admits the Canadian without a B-1 I-94 or any other documentation. The maximum period of stay is six months.

Use B-1 Visas Only In Special Cases

Because of uncertain results at ports of entry, I recommend B-1 visas only in special cases. When in doubt, try to obtain longer-term nonimmigrant working visas. B-1 visas often involve borderline situations where no clear definition of "work" exists. Most of us think we work during a business trip. But under a B-1 visa, you cannot work. It's easy to get confused and it's easy for INS to misapply the rules based on your confusion.

Before applying for a B-1 visa consider that you may also qualify for a longer-term nonimmigrant work visa. It might be worth paying U.S. taxes to know there'll be no trouble entering the U.S. The time, expense and disruption to your business resulting from being delayed or refused entry to the U.S. may exceed the costs associated with a nonimmigrant working visa.

In summary, B-1 provides more certain results than visa waiver, and a nonimmigrant visa provides more certain results than B-1.

Chapter 4

The B-2 Visa — How to Travel for Pleasure

Since the advent of the visa waiver program, fewer people need B-2 Visitor for Pleasure visas. (Visa waivers are available for people from Canada, most European countries, and Japan.) After all, how many people take vacations that last more than two weeks, let alone more than the 90 days permitted under visa waiver?

If you are eligible for a visa waiver, consuls usually will not issue a B-2 visa. Normally, families or couples coming to the U.S. for short vacations or even for a summer tour face few problems entering on visa waiver or obtaining B-2 visas. The B-2 application procedures are the same as for B-1 visas.

Problems with Single Young Adults, Parents & Students

Single young men and women and student-age children face intense scrutiny when applying for a B-2 visa, or when applying for permission to enter the U.S. Student-age children come to the U.S. with or without parents—often posing as tourists—with the intention of enrolling in school. Mothers often stay in the U.S. illegally to take care of the child. No visa category permits mothers to care for children going to American schools. This scenario, aside from being illegal, often burdens the American public education and welfare systems.

Students

If a child enters the U.S. as a tourist without an endorsed visa and later attempts to change to student status, the INS may find that the child misrepresented his intentions for entering the U.S. and deny the change of B-2 to F-1 student status request. Even if the INS approves the change of status from B-2 to F-1 student and subsequently the student applies for a visa, most consuls will resist issuing an F-1 student visa for the same reasons. This will mean that the student cannot leave the U.S. to apply for a visa with any assurance of being able to return. Students often find themselves "locked" within the U.S., separated from their families, while holding an illegal visa that will expire well before the school term is completed.

Student-age children intending to enroll in an American school should tell the consul the truth. If convinced of a child's student bonafides and financial support, the consul will issue a B-2 visa endorsed "Prospective Student," or the like. Such an endorsement permits the children and parents to find a suitable school for the student. If all goes well, the child may change to F-1 status while in the U.S., and later return home to apply for an F-1 student visa. Effective documentation for prospective F-1 students using a B-2 visa to shop for schools includes:

- Academic references
- A list of prospective schools
- Letters of invitation to visit schools
- Proof of arrangements for care and support while attending school in the U.S.

Young Adults

Young single men and women face a different problem. Many singles come to the U.S. for no other purpose than to marry their way to a green card. The high incidence of singles coming to the U.S. for this reason has influenced INS enforcement policy. Unfortunately, this policy creates difficulties for young singles who have legitimate reasons for visiting the U.S.

Yet there are ways for young singles to come to the U.S. for legitimate travel reasons. It's important that they carefully document plans to return home following a vacation. Effective documentation includes:

- Proof of a job or business at home
- Proof of family ties at home (list family members)

- Proof that you are pursuing an education at home
- A detailed itinerary of the U.S. trip
- Letters of invitation or reference from U.S. citizens or permanent residents
- Proof that you can support yourself while in the U.S.

In other words, provide proof that you have too much to lose by leaving home for an extended period.

Chapter 5

Temporary Working Visas

International organizations and corporations use nonimmigrant working visas to staff U.S. operations. Investors use nonimmigrant visas for themselves and employees sent to the U.S. to monitor investments. U.S. employers use nonimmigrant visas to fill skill shortages in their companies.

Many people use nonimmigrant working visas as a stepping stone to permanent residence status and then citizenship. People commonly obtain a nonimmigrant work visa so they can remain in the U.S. while applying or waiting for a green card.

This chapter defines the basic terms and concepts concerning the most commonly used nonimmigrant work visas: E, H and L. Subsequent chapters describe less frequently used categories along with the strategy and approach for specific situations.

General

The U.S. maintains two interdependent nonimmigrant working visa systems. E visas are the product of treaties, negotiated between the U.S. and other countries and administered by the Department of State through embassies and consulates. Congress created the other commonly used nonimmigrant work visas (H and L) through domestic law. The INS serves as the lead agency for administering H and L visas or other visas created by domestic law. Read this chapter before the other chapters that discuss how to staff companies, make investments in the U.S., or obtain a green card.

Most companies use a combination of E-1/2, H-1B, L-1A and L-1B visas to staff their U.S. operations. The same person may qualify for an E visa category or an H or L visa category. The combination of the H and L categories describes the same work activities as the E categories. E visas include professionals, managers, executives and essential skill employees, whereas H and L include professionals, executives, managers and specialized knowledge employees. Differences in corporate ownership and organization, convenience, or the enforcement policies of the initial governmental agency you'll be working with—the INS or Department of State—determine whether to apply for an E visa or an H or L visa.

Terminology

Professionals

The term "professional" refers to four-year university graduates who work in professional positions. These include lawyers, accountants, economists, engineers, market researchers and economists. Depending on individual circumstances, a professional may qualify for H-1B status, E status, or even L-1A manager status.

Executive/Manager

The term "executive" utilizes its literal meaning. The term "manager" refers to someone who directs or monitors the activities of other professionals, managers and supervisors. Managers are not involved in the direct manufacture of a product or provision of a service. Most executives and managers use E or L-1A manager visas.

International Organization

The term "international organization" refers to U.S. companies having 50 percent or more common ownership with a foreign company or individuals. Ownership may be traced through unlimited tiers of companies or individuals as long as one can ultimately establish 50 percent or more common ownership.

Essential Skill & Specialized Knowledge

"Essential skill" (E visa) or "specialized knowledge" (L-1B visa) applicants possess knowledge critical to the success of the U.S. (E visa) or beneficial to U.S. competitiveness (L-1B visa). When essential skills or specialized knowledge applicants also serve in executive/managerial or professional positions, they may also qualify for H-1B, L-1A or E visa status as professionals or executive/managers.

L Visas: Intra-Company Transference

The L visa category includes executive, manager or specialized knowledge applicants who transfer within an international organization. To qualify for any L category, the visa applicant must transfer within the same international organization. The applicant must work in a qualifying capacity (as an executive, manager or specialized knowledge employee) for a foreign member of the international organization, for one of the three years preceding the transfer to the American member of the international organization in the same capacity. L visa applicants file Form I-129 and the L supplement with the INS.

As an example, a manager joined the foreign parent company in 1991 and resigned in June 1993. In June 1994 the foreign parent company rehired the manager to transfer to the U.S., then filed its L-1A petition. The manager meets the one-year test because he worked as a manager in the foreign parent company one of the three years prior to the petition filing date. If the applicant fails the one-year requirement, consider E or H-1B visa status.

To qualify as an international organization, the parent company must establish a branch office, subsidiary company or affiliate company in the U.S. From an immigration point of view, it makes little difference whether a branch, subsidiary or affiliated company is formed as long as the arrangement qualifies as an international organization for L-1 purposes. International organizations are as follows.

Branch Office in the U.S.

A branch office refers to the parent company registering itself to do business in the U.S., as opposed to forming a subsidiary or affiliate.

Subsidiary Company

A subsidiary for L visa purposes is a U.S. company owned 50 percent or more by a foreign corporation.

Affiliated Company

An affiliated company is a business linked by at least 50 percent common ownership to the foreign parent. For L-1 purposes the foreign parent must directly or indirectly control the U.S. branch, subsidiary or affiliate. "Control" in this case generally means 50 percent or more direct or indirect ownership.

A 50-50 joint venture between a foreign and American company may be an affiliate of the foreign company since the foreign company owns half of the U.S. business. The joint venture could be a partnership between the U.S. company and the foreign company's wholly-owned U.S. subsidiary. Or it could be a corporation half owned by U.S. shareholders or companies, and half by the foreign company or its subsidiary. Many foreign companies transfer managers, executives or specialized knowledge persons to U.S. joint-venture operations.

Treaty Trader/Investor—Basic Terminology

The following discussion involves the workings of the treaty trader/investor treaties. It's difficult to understand how to use E visas without some background on the subject.

The E categories include executive, managers, professional and essential skill applicants hired by a company controlled by at least 50 percent of the treaty nationals involved in qualifying trade or investment. The E visa applicant must be of the same nationality as the controlling ownership. The American E visa employer qualifies as a treaty company on the basis of the nationality of its shareholders as well as the qualifying trade or investment.

E Visa Processing

E visa processing consists of two basic steps. First, the U.S. company must be qualified as a Treaty Trader or Treaty Investor. The U.S. company must prove it made a substantial investment or controls substantial qualifying trade. Secondly, the company must prove the applicant qualifies as an executive, manager or essential skill employee.

The applicant, if in the U.S., may change to E status by filing for an INS change of status on Form I-129, Application for Nonimmigrant Workers, with the E supplement. If the applicant works abroad, the application must be filed with a consul. Forms, procedures and enforcement policies vary among the consular offices.

The treaty national employees of a treaty trader company receive E-1 visas. The treaty national employees of a treaty investor company obtain E-2 visas. When the same company qualifies for both E-1 and E-2 status, the consul will only accord the applicant one status. For example, Taiwan is a "treaty country," thus making a Taiwanese-controlled company in the U.S. a "treaty company" and a Taiwanese citizen working for the treaty company a "treaty national."

Note that green card holders count as U.S. workers for E visa purposes regardless of their nationality. In the above example, a Taiwanese green card holder may not qualify as a treaty national as he or she is considered a "U.S. person."

The Treaties

The "treaty" refers to a Friendship Commerce and Navigation Treaty (FCN), or a Bilateral Investment Treaty (BIT) between the U.S. and a foreign country. Such treaties contain agreements concerning trade, investing, shipping, aviation and staffing of operations in each country. The U.S. has negotiated such treaties with over 50 countries, including Japan, Taiwan, Korea, Thailand, most European countries, and Canada.

The U.S. originally negotiated FCN and BIT treaties to assure equal access to foreign markets and prevent arbitrary limitations on the number of treaty nationals permitted to staff foreign operations. Now that the U.S. runs a trade deficit, FCN and BIT treaties tend to protect foreign nationals doing business in the U.S. Twenty-five years ago, the reverse was true.

Many countries created arbitrary ratios (such as one American technician per five Japanese technicians) to assure local control of foreign enterprises. FCN and BIT treaties prevented this practice by giving treaty traders or investors the opportunity to staff foreign operations with qualified persons of their "choice."

Although there is no legal limit on the number of E visa employees, over the years the State Department limited the treaty company's "choice" by imposing training requirements, suggesting that treaty companies hire more

U.S. workers, or by strictly defining the classes of eligible workers. Today, "choice" means that the treaty company may employ as many applicants as it wants as long as the consul agrees.

Control & Ownership of a U.S. Treaty Company

"Control" refers to 50 percent or more treaty national ownership of a U.S. company. Japan is a treaty country, and a joint venture based in the U.S. and controlled by 50 percent or more of Japanese treaty nationals qualifies as a treaty company. U.S. subsidiaries of companies such as Sony and Honda are treaty companies. Public companies generally take the nationality of their primary place of incorporation or the location of the stock exchange that trades most of their shares.

Subsequent changes in corporate ownership by either the parent or U.S. treaty company may affect treaty status. Treaty nationals must at all times control the U.S. treaty company. If at any time treaty national ownership dips below 50 percent, the U.S. treaty company loses its treaty status. Fifty-fifty joint ventures risk losing treaty status if U.S. shareholders purchase addititional shares from the treaty national shareholders, thus changing the ownership ratio.

Treaty Trader: E-1 Visa

Service and trading companies may qualify for E-1 treaty trader status. "Trade" signifies trade in goods and trade in services. Banks, financial-service companies, software firms, attorneys, accountants, and the like, along with companies trading goods, may qualify for E-1 treaty trader status.

"Treaty Trade" means substantial trade primarily between the treaty national countries. "Primarily" means that

50 percent or more of the treaty company trade (the U.S. operation) is between the treaty company and the treaty country. If Honda USA wants to be a treaty trader company, over half of its imports and exports must be between the U.S. and Japan.

Treaty Trade must be substantial, though there is no specific monetary amount to define "substantial." Enforcement varies among U.S. consuls world-wide as local economic conditions dictate the definition of substantial treaty trade.

In Japan, Taiwan, Korea and Europe, substantial trade generally involves many small annual transactions of at least $500,000, or a few large annual transactions in the millions of dollars. In lesser developed countries, consuls often approve E-1 visas for smaller amounts of trade. Generally, the poorer the country the lower the trade threshold. Consuls focus on business activity and try to limit treaty trader status to active and on-going business ventures, not short-term projects.

Direct Trade

Only direct trade qualifies for E-1 purposes. For example, U.S.-incorporated Japanese treaty Company A sells to U.S.-incorporated Japanese treaty Company B. Company B exports to Japan. Company A cannot claim B's exports for E-1 trade purposes even if the Japanese buyer is A's parent company. If Company A wants E-1 status, it must make sure the exports are shipped under its name.

Trade Primarily Between the U.S. & a Treaty Country

Trade between the U.S. and a treaty country must exceed 50 percent of the U.S. treaty company's total worldwide trade. "Trade" is defined by the U.S. treaty company's commerce with a treaty country. In one case, a Taiwanese company exports from the U.S. to Taiwan through a branch office in America. As the U.S. dollar lost value, trade between the U.S. and Taiwan fell to less than 50 percent of the company's total trade. Because of this drop in trade the company lost its E-1 visa status.

Doing business in the U.S. through a U.S.-incorporated subsidiary prevents the above scenario. A branch office is part of the parent company, not a separate company. Thus the parent is also the treaty company. A branch office must compare its trade with the treaty country to the parent company's total world-wide trade. A U.S. subsidiary is a separate company, not part of the parent company. In the case of a subsidiary company, "treaty trade" refers to the subsidiary company's trade with the treaty country. As long as the U.S. subsidiary does 50 percent or more of its import/export business with the treaty country (not necessarily the parent company), the trade will be primarily between the U.S. and the treaty country.

Treaty Investor E-2

E-2 status requires a substantial treaty investment. A "substantial investment" in a business generally involves at least $200,000. Payment may be in cash or a combination of cash and debt. Depending on national conditions and individual circumstances, the U.S. Consulate may approve cases for smaller ventures. Although there is no statutory minimum investment, the smaller the investment the tougher it is to get visa approval. Funds must come from the treaty country of the investor, and borrowed funds may not be secured by assets of the treaty investment.

The smaller the cost of the business, the higher the percentage of cash investment required. Consular officers usually require a cash investment of 65 percent, or $130,000, for a business that costs $200,000. A million-dollar investment requires a smaller investment percentage. Again, these are only general guidelines. Consuls base their decisions on the specific facts of each case.

Basic Requirements of H Visas: For Professional Workers

The applicant must have professional qualifications and work in a job requiring these qualifications. For example, a staff economist should have a Bachelor of Arts degree in Economics. The term "specialty worker" used in the regulations really means "professional worker." If the applicant does not have a university degree, don't pursue H-1B visa status. The regulations exempt people with 10 or more years of work experience from the degree requirement. However, if there's another visa choice, use it. Qualifying for H-1B status without a university degree is very difficult.

The U.S. government limits the number of H-1B visas to 65,000 per year. So far, the limit has never been reached and there is no indication that the limit will be reached in the near future.

H-1B Employer

H-1B employers may be completely U.S.-owned, completely foreign-owned, or a combination of the two. An H-1B employer must be incorporated or otherwise licensed to do business in the U.S., i.e. an American employer. An American employer, or a U.S. agent of a foreign employer, must petition for H-1B and L status. Foreign employers may petition for E status. The term "U.S. Employer" refers to the place of incorporation or licensure, not ownership.

A totally foreign-owned U.S. corporation is a U.S. employer because it is incorporated in the U.S.

The Labor Conditions Application Process

H-1B employers must file a Labor Conditions Application (LCA) form with the U.S. Department of Labor, post the form on the company bulletin board for 10 days, or give the form to a union representative prior to filing for H-1B. The LCA form requires the employer to disclose the H-1B applicant's job title and salary to ensure there is no labor problem, and to promise to pay the H-1B applicant the prevailing wage. The LCA procedures add approximately 30 days to H-1B visa processing. Only after LCA approval may employers petition the INS for H-1B status. Allow 45 days for H-1B processing, in addition to the LCA processing.

"Prevailing Wage" is the salary that the Department of Labor determines most people in the work area earn for a particular job. Employers must document how they determined the prevailing wage. It's best to obtain a prevailing wage determination from the State Department of Labor before filing an H-1B petition.

Given current dollar exchange rates, Japanese or European companies rarely fail to pay the prevailing wage. On top of the exchange-rate benefits, foreign companies transferring an employee to the U.S. must usually increase the transferee's wages to entice him to move his family to the U.S. American companies looking for low-priced foreign labor often have trouble with the prevailing wage rate.

Many companies resist telling U.S. workers the salary of a new foreign worker. However, the Department of Labor may levy fines—and/or prohibit the employer from applying for H-1B visas—for not posting the LCA notice where all employees can see it, failing to disclose accurate information, or not paying the prevailing wage.

The LCA requirement is unavoidable, with the only alternative to use another visa category. However, you don't always have that choice.

Professional Licenses

H-1B professionals must either be licensed in the state of intended employment or be exempt from the license requirement. State law defines the professions which require a license. In most cases, professionals such as engineers, lawyers, accountants or architects, who work for a company and do not serve the public, don't require state licenses. One must consult state law to determine licensure requirements.

As an example, companies often transfer a person to oversee the legal matters of their U.S. operations. In many countries, universities offer an undergraduate program in commercial law. Commonly, graduates never take a bar exam or obtain a license to practice law. In-house lawyers or businessmen with law degrees qualify for H-1B status.

The typical applicant usually holds a commercial law degree and has worked with the company's benefit programs, labor relations, regulatory compliance, or contractual negotiations. The applicant never took a license to practice law. The applicant will be transferred to the U.S subsidiary to coordinate subsidiary and home-office legal affairs, monitor regulatory compliance, engage outside professionals on an as-needed basis, coordinate home-office and subsidiary benefit plans, and monitor compliance with U.S. civil rights antidiscrimination rules. This applicant doesn't need a license to practice law because he serves his company, not the public.

When to Use H, L or E

Corporate organization, convenience, or the applicant's background may dictate whether to apply for E, H or L categories. Each of the E, H and L categories permit the applicant to work in the U.S. and allow spouses and children to live or study (but not work) in the U.S. Dependent children must be under age 21. Children over age 21 need an independent visa status. All three categories are employer-specific. The holder of the visa may only work for the sponsoring employer.

Assuming you may choose between E, H or L status, consider the following guidelines:

- E visas may be extended as long as the U.S. business remains viable. There is no limit to extensions of the visa. Most consuls issue E visas for five-year periods.

- L visas are limited to seven years for executives and managers and five years for specialized knowledge. H visas are limited to six years for professionals. Most initial L-1 and H-1B visas are valid for three years.

- If you ultimately want a green card, try to arrange your affairs so that you are transferred in a managerial or executive capacity within an international organization.

- If none of the above matters to you, apply for the category that affords the fastest and easiest processing. This depends on a comparison of the enforcement policies and service standards of the consulate nearest your home to those of the INS service center controlling the area of your intended employment.

Summary of Eligibility for E, H & L Visa Holders

L visas accommodate transfers within an international organization, and E visas accommodate citizens or companies of the treaty country involved in qualifying trade or investment. H-1B professionals may work for any incorporated or licensed U.S. company that requires the services of a professional. The definitions overlap and the same person may qualify for one or more visa categories.

The following scenarios clarify company requirements for the E, H and L visas. If the U.S. employer is:

• A member of an L visa international organization and qualifies for either E-1 or E-2 status, the company may utilize L, H and E visas.

• Not a member of an L visa international organization but qualifies for either E-1 or E-2 status, the company may use E or H visas.

• Not a member of an L visa international organization, and does not qualify for E-1 or E-2 status, the company may only use H visas.

In rare cases, consider O, P and Q visas. See Chapter 10.

Chapter 6

Staffing for a New Business in America

This chapter describes how to staff a low-capital start-up company with H-1B or L-1A visas. Initially, most start-up companies send a person to the U.S. to conduct market research and establish the first office.

At this point there is usually no trade or investment. Because treaty investments require substantial capital outlay, and treaty trade requires substantial trade, fledgling businesses rarely qualify for treaty status. If the parent company capitalizes the U.S. branch or subsidiary, consider utilizing E visas for employees.

Establish the U.S. Company First

The first step in setting up a U.S. business is to establish a legal entity licensed to do business in a particular state. If possible, see that the U.S. company qualifies as an international organization for L-1 visa purposes. Otherwise, you may be restricted to H-1B visas or have to make a qualified treaty investment.

Incorporating a company in the U.S. is a simple matter; there is no requirement for a U.S. or federal company registration. Incorporate at the state level, and not with the federal government in Washington D.C. Most states use similar rules and procedures. No states conduct background checks or impose minimum capital requirements. Foreigners may serve as officers or directors without restriction. Officers and directors do not have to reside in the state of incorporation. Additionally, apply for a federal tax identification (ID) number as well as state and local business licenses. It only takes a few weeks and about $1,000 in legal and license fees to form a corporation or register a branch office.

Have a Premise for Doing Business

The U.S. company must rent or own a place of business. It is not advisable to use an apartment or a house as the first office. If the INS recognizes a residential address, it will question your intent to do business in the U.S. After all, why would any government grant a work visa to a cottage industry or a person operating an office out of a home? What is the benefit to U.S. employment?

The Visa Application

Once an office is established you can apply for the L-1A or H-1B visa. Most companies use L-1A visas. The L-1A visa permits a manager to come to the U.S. for an initial period of one year to help establish the start-up enterprise. Although other visa categories may also accomplish similar results, the L-1A was designed to accommodate start-up situations. The foreign parent company must convince the INS that they have sufficient capital and experience to support the fledgling U.S. business. The visa applicant must be a managerial or executive employee who worked for your corporate group for one of the three years prior to the petition date.

A Case Study

The following is a case study of the visa requirements for a new U.S. business.

A foreign chemical company plans to enter the U.S. market. It already sells products through a U.S. distributor, and wants to establish a U.S. subsidiary to ultimately purchase the distributor and establish sales and manufacturing operations in the U.S.

The transfer candidate, a 35-year-old manager with 10 years experience with the parent company, will be the only employee during the start-up period. The candidate manages export sales to the U.S. for the parent company, and has worked with the U.S. distributor. While working in the U.S. the candidate will conduct market research and prepare for the takeover of the distributor. The foreign company leases office space from the distributor and has established a U.S. subsidiary corporation.

This should be a textbook case of proper eligibility. There is a qualified manager, a parent company with money and experience, and a reasonable business plan. After much deliberation, the INS approves the case.

The INS scrutinizes applications for start-up companies as they often fail to demonstrate the financial ability to support a new U.S. business. To help prove financial responsibility the parent company often sends money to the new U.S. office. It also helps to show enough liquid assets to support the new business. If possible, the parent company should show proof of successfully establishing foreign offices in other countries.

Alternatives to the L-1A Approach: E-2 & H-1B

We could have approached the case study in two other ways. Assuming appropriate treaty nationality, the parent company could have capitalized the U.S. subsidiary and signed a letter of intent to purchase the U.S. distributor. The capital transfer (depending upon the amount), coupled with the letter of intent, should permit one E-2 manager to come to the U.S. to establish the new company.

The H-1B visa provides an interesting alternative to the L-1A visa for start-up companies. Employees with a professional level of education (university degree) who come to work in a professional position for a U.S. employer, qualify for H-1B status. A subsidiary of a foreign company incorporated in the U.S. qualifies as a U.S. employer. Start-up companies applying for an H-1B visa must prove sufficient capital to support the new employee and his activities.

The first person to staff the start-up usually conducts market research and formulates the plan for launching the business. Depending upon the scope of the project, market research often requires professional expertise. Bachelor of arts degrees in marketing, business, commercial law, economics, political science, accounting and finance logically support market research or business planning positions. In technical areas, market research may require an engineering or other scientific degree.

The-H-1B visa provides two advantages over L-1A in the start-up situation. The INS usually issues the initial H-1 visa for three years, not an initial one-year period as in the L-1A, and there is no requirement to hire employees as in the case of the L-1A.

Most people prefer using L-1A to H-1B because the L-1 regulations specifically accommodate start-up situations, and it's easier to obtain a green card starting from L-1A status. Start-ups use H-1B when there's some doubt about L-1A eligibility.

After a One-Year Period

NOTE: New legislation may impose gross sales and investment requirements on L-1A companies. For example, a start-up L-1 company may have to show minimum annualized gross sales of, say, $300,000 per year at the end of the first year of operation and/or a minimum investment of, say, $200,000. This means that the sales trend should show that the company is on the path to minimum gross sales of $300,000.

Start-up company L-1A visas have an initial validity period of one year, not three years as in other L-1 situations. The L-1A manager must conduct active business and hire employees within the one-year period. Remember, L-1 managers must oversee other employees. At a minimum, the manager must make tangible progress toward establishing the business. At the end of the first year the L-1A visa can be extended for up to two three-year periods.

Normally, H-1B visa holders are limited to six-year consecutive stays, while L-1A visa holders are restricted to a seven-year consecutive stay. At the end of the validity period they may change to any status other than H or L (perhaps E status), or must leave the U.S. for a year before reapplying for a H-1B or L-1A visa.

L-1A visa renewals become difficult without the manager making tangible progress in conducting active U.S. business. Well-capitalized companies fare better in this regard as they can say their lack of progress is due to larger projects which take more time to launch. And they can easily prove they have the capital necessary to continue the project. Small companies often must reapply as a start-up or change to H-1B status. E visas will not work without active trade or a substantial investment, in which case there should be no problem extending the L-1A.

The INS designed the one-year "doing business" requirement to force the applicant company to show good-faith efforts in establishing itself in the U.S. In the 1980s many Taiwanese companies established U.S. subsidiaries as "shell" companies. Their purpose was to move children to the U.S. for educational purposes and ultimately to obtain green cards. The INS has since taken steps to curtail such abuse of the rules.

The one-year of doing business rule technically considers mitigating circumstances, such as some businesses taking longer than others to establish. A business may also encounter bad luck or unforeseen delays. The INS tends to take a simplistic view. After one year, if there are no employees and the gross sales are low, no visa extension will be issued.

Once the business is established, managers may consider changing to E visa status. There is no reason to change to an E visa unless you will be staying in the U.S. longer than six years, or unless you have children under the age of 21 attending a state university. Many state universities offer lower-cost resident tuition to E visa dependents, whereas L and H visa dependents will pay the more expensive nonresident tuitions.

Dependent Children

Children may use the principal alien's visa status until the age of 21. Spouses and children receive H-4 or L-2 visas. E visa dependents receive the same designation as the principal alien endorsed as the dependent. Spouses and children may not work in the U.S. without a visa that specifically authorizes employment. Dependent status does not authorize employment. After age 21, children must obtain an independent visa.

Many foreign young people are in university when they turn 21, and at that time, change to F-1 student status. Children with an F-1 student visa cannot work except for a one-year period of practical training or in other on-campus programs. At some point the child will graduate. After graduation, adult children must change from F-1 student status to another category, or return home.

Dependents over 21 years of age cannot work or stay in the U.S. for the long term without getting married to a U.S. citizen, or finding a job that leads to a visa. As a result, some parents obtain green cards before the children reach age 21. The green card petition includes children under the age of 21. A green card permits children to remain in the U.S. without parents and to freely study and work in the U.S. State universities treat green card holders as residents eligible for the less costlier resident tuitions.

As you can see, there are several approaches used in start-up business situations. Use the approach that best suits your long-term goals, and the one that fits your business and personal plans.

Chapter 7

Staffing an Existing U.S. Business

Now that we have described how to staff a start-up enterprise, let's look at staffing existing businesses.

This chapter discusses:

- Treaty trader or treaty investor E-1 and E-2
- L-1A Manager
- L-1B Specialized Knowledge
- H-1B Professional visas
- H-2B Seasonal Workers or Labor Unavailable in the U.S.

Choosing the Correct Visa

Each visa category presents advantages and disadvantages. Consuls generally process E visa petitions faster than the INS processes H and L visa petitions. L-1A visas work better than other categories in start-up situations. H-1B petitions require LCA disclosures. The LCA disclosure entails additional processing time and may disturb relations with U.S. workers. L-1B visas tend to require detailed explanations of the applicant's benefit to U.S. competitiveness, while L-1A visas tend to require detailed explanations of the company's organization and the applicant's managerial duties.

The E-1/2 essential skill category requires that the U.S. company trains replacements. The H-2B category requires recruitment of U.S. workers. H and L visas have maximum validity periods, while E visas may be extended indefinitely. On the other hand, H-1B, L-1A, L-1B and E visas all permit the applicant to work in the U.S., while allowing dependents to live and attend school in America.

Managers

Companies hire an endless variety of managers and executives, including administrative managers, human resource managers, accounting managers, production managers, company officers, sales managers, etc. Simply put, managers tell other people what to do.

Managers working for an international organization may qualify for L-1A Manager, E-1/2 Manager, or H-1B Manager serving in a professional capacity. Managers working for a treaty company that isn't part of an international organization qualify for E-1/2 or H-1B. If the company isn't a treaty organization or an international organization, H-1B Professional status becomes the only choice. Treaty organizations or international organizations may pay managers from abroad. In such cases, the U.S. employer must remit payroll tax and income tax withholding to the IRS for wages earned in the U.S.

Managers may commute between foreign and American locations. If questioned, the manager must demonstrate that he performs managerial duties while in the U.S. It's not how much time the manager spends in the U.S., it's what the manager does while there.

Corporate organization will either expand or limit your choices. Assuming you have all three choices—H-1B, L-1A and E-1/2, consider the following points.

Factors Favoring E Visas

- In most cases, consuls process visas faster than INS.
- E visa holders receive up to two-year stay periods every time they enter the U.S. An E visa holder entering the U.S. on the last day of his visa may be admitted for up to two years beyond the visa expiration date.
- L or H visa holders will only be admitted for a period not longer than their visa validity date. Depending on the circumstances, the E visa may eliminate the need to file an extension petition with the INS.

- The E visa may theoretically be extended indefinitely, whereas the H visa is limited to six years and L-1A visa is limited to seven years.

- If the company is replacing an E visa holder with a person serving the same position, use the E visa category for the replacement. By granting the E visa the first time the consul has already determined that the position qualifies.

Factors Favoring H & L Visas

- Consuls usually review the U.S. employer's staffing history. Consuls generally resist granting E visas for more than one person per position. The INS only reviews the case in front of them, and usually doesn't review the entire company's staffing structure and visa history. For example, if you think there will be trouble justifying the need for more than one sales manager, use the L-1A or H-1B categories.

- Consuls tend to question E visa petitions for managers under 30 years of age. In such cases, if the manager also has a professional degree, consider H-1B or L-1A.

- If your company frequently uses E visas and cannot demonstrate a declining ratio of foreign versus American workers, consider H and L visas for new positions.

Determining the correct visa is more of an art than a science. One must consider long-term staffing goals. If your company plans to rotate managers between the U.S. and foreign offices, it's important to establish precedents with the INS and consuls for all possible categories.

If hiring a foreign manager is an infrequent or one-time situation, use the visa category that best suits the applicant's credentials and long-term goals. For example, if the applicant may ultimately want a green card and the U.S. employer is part of an international organization, use the E or L-1A categories. As you will see in the next chapter, changing to a green card from an H-1B visa can be difficult.

Unless you ultimately want a green card, there is little practical difference between any of these visa categories. Choose the category that facilitates staffing the U.S. business in the quickest and smoothest way possible. Applicants often qualify for several visa categories, and it is important to match the job requirements and applicant's skills with the most appropriate category. The closer the match, the faster the processing.

H-1B Visas

The H-1B visa is the preferable visa category for professionals. Professional positions include most jobs that require a baccalaureate or higher degree as a minimum requirement. These could include accountants, engineers, economists, teachers, scientists, market researchers, sales engineers, psychiatrists, dieticians, foresters, hotel managers, librarians, journalists, medical doctors, minsiters, nutritionists, pharmacists, sociologists, lawyers, veterinarians, vocational counselors, fashion models, technical publications writers, and social workers.

The H-1B visa category offers simplicity. If the job requires a professional and the applicant has the appropriate professional background, the visa will be approved. Although U.S. workers must be notified of the impending H-1B petition, there is no requirement to recruit or hire U.S. workers. There is also no requirement that the applicant have experience in the job offered. Recent college graduates often qualify for H-1B status. On the downside, the notification procedure, Labor Conditions Attestation, though relatively simple, requires additional processing time.

H-1B petitions require information about the applicant's professional abilities, the employer's need for a professional to fill the offered position, the applicant's resume, and educational credentials.

The size of the employer makes little difference in clearly professional positions, such as engineers and accountants. Small companies often have trouble justifying the need for a professional to fill marketing and administrative positions. For example, a small company has little need for the permanent services of a market researcher. The INS might suspect that the "market researcher" who holds an economics or marketing degree is really a salesman.

Small companies generally don't need professionals—such as Business Administration degree holders—to fill administrative positions. Most small business managers learn on the job. A baccalaureate degree is usually not a job requirement for the small company's business adminstrator or manager. Large companies with complex management structures fare better in demonstrating the need for business adminstration, MBA, or other business-related degree holders.

Common Applications of H-1 Visas

Financial & Business Professionals

Foreign-owned companies often transfer financial and accounting professionals to oversee cost-containment, the purchase of raw materials or parts, preparation of financial reports for the home office, and general accounting and financial activities. Typically the transferee lacks managerial experience and the job in the U.S. rarely contains a managerial component. The lack of managerial experience eliminates any managerial visa possibilities.

As finance-related skills are widely available in the U.S. and usually don't aid U.S. competitiveness, L-1B specialized knowledge or E-1/2 essential skill visas are not recommended for these employees. H-1B status for finance and accounting positions is recommended for four reasons:

- The work falls within established professional disciplines.

- The services of a professional are required to understand financial, accounting or procurement systems.

- The applicant generally has an appropriate university degree (finance, economics or business administration).

- There is no requirement to demonstrate a shortage of U.S. workers or that U.S. workers cannot perform the job.

A typical job description for an economist, accountant or financial officer might be as follows.

"Prepare financial reports, budgets, analyze operating results as compared to budget projections, coordinate home office and subsidiary accounting methods, monitor cost control, prepare and analyze forecasts for executive management, work with outside professionals regarding tax return preparation and financial reporting."

Engineers

We recommend H-1B visas for nonmanagerial engineers or scientists (mechanical, electrical and computer engineers, etc.) because engineering is a recognized profession usually requiring a related university degree.

Sales engineers often pose difficult cases. Is the sales

engineer a salesman or an engineer? Sales managers may qualify for L-1A or E visas; salesmen do not qualify for any visa category. The typical sales engineer holds an engineering-related university degree, works on product development and design, and provides technical support to customers. The sales engineer explains the product in layman's terms.

Companies that manufacture or sell complicated products in the U.S. hire sales engineers to "explain the product to the customer, provide technical support to company salesmen, interface with the customer's engineers and technicians, provide customer technical support, and, after warranty service, work with customer's engineers and technicians regarding product modification, and install and monitor maintenance programs."

This job description describes sales activity. But the sales engineer also requires technical expertise and a theoretical understanding of the product's mechanics, hence the engineering background. A successful H-1B petition hinges on emphasizing the technical aspects of the job. Stress the technical or professional understanding of the product required to make the sale, rather than the salesmanship angle.

NOTE: It's possible that in the future Congress may impose minimum experience requirements on H-1B workers. For example, Congress may require three years of professional experience abroad. This means that recent college graduates would not qualify. Currently, there is no minimum experience requirement for H-1B workers.

Summary

Use H-1B when managerial visas are inappropriate and the applicant has a four-year degree relating to a professional discipline. Liberal arts degrees in such areas as literature, business administration, English or other languages are problematic because the degrees rarely relate directly to the job offered.

The H-1B category presents three disadvantages. The duration is limited to six years; it's difficult to go from H-1B to green card status; and the employer must go through the LCA procedure. Therefore, use the H-1B visa category in the following circumstances:

- The corporate organization makes the H-1B the only choice.

- If there are choices, use the H-1B if the applicant is young and has little experience and a qualifying BA degree.

Specialized Knowledge & Essential Skills

Companies often transfer specialists who work with a particular product, technology or process. Specialists may qualify for four visa categories: E-1/2 Essential Skill, L-1B Specialized Knowledge, H-1B Professional, or H-2B Labor Unavailable in the U.S.

If the applicant earned a university degree related to his specialty, we recommend H-1B. Such an applicant, for example, would have a Bachelor of Science degree in Fisheries for marine-products specialist, Computer Science degree for computer/software specialist, and Forestry degree for wood products specialist.

It is easier to prove that the university degree relates to the applicant's specialty than to prove the applicant's skills are essential to the U.S. enterprise (E visa), or an aid to U.S. competitiveness (L-1B). An H-1B visa works because the applicant must use professional skills to understand, modify or analyze a complex product, technology or process.

If a specialist lacks a university degree but holds skills unavailable in the U.S. necessary to the company's success, consider E-1 Essential Skills status. If the specialized skill helps promote U.S. trade or exports, the applicant may qualify for L-1B Specialized Knowledge status. Since both categories face equally intense scrutiny, choose the category that best matches the facts of the case.

L-1B and E-1/2 essential skills refer to the same sorts of skills but with a different emphasis. "Essential skills" refer to skills critical to the U.S. company's success. In other words, the success of a U.S. business depends upon the applicant's essential skills. Additionally, the essential skills in question must be unavailable in the U.S. The U.S. treaty company usually must agree to train people to replace the essential skills' applicant.

For example, it's often impossible to effectively utilize foreign machinery without the temporary services of a technician who provides training and technical support. American technicians are unfamiliar with the newly introduced machinery, so the U.S. treaty company must agree to train technicians from the U.S.

Specialized knowledge refers to skills or knowledge of the parent company's product or processes which must be transferred to the U.S. subsidiary for increasing the subsidiary company's competitiveness. The emphasis is on helping U.S. competitiveness, not the necessity or scarcity of the skill. Although the U.S. produces many software engineers, the installation of the parent company's particular software in the U.S. subsidiary may aid the U.S. subsidiary's competitiveness in international markets.

Who Can Use L-1B & E Essential Skill Visas

There's an endless list of appropriate applications for the L-1B and E essential skills visas. In general, use this category for persons with technical skills but who lack university degrees. Some points to remember:

- Use another category unless the applicant doesn't qualify as an international manager or have a professional degree. Professionals and managers may also hold specialized knowledge or essential skills.

- The consuls and INS scrutinize L-1 specialized knowledge cases and E essential skills cases more than managerial or professional cases.

- Use L-1 specialized knowledge when transferring knowledge which helps U.S. competitiveness. The knowledge does not have to be secret or proprietary. On the other hand, if everyone has this knowledge how can it aid U.S. competitiveness? A lot of companies make instant noodles, but not everyone's instant noodles taste the same. The knowledge that makes Company A's noodles taste different than its competitor's is specialized.

- Use E essential skill status when the emphasis is on training U.S. labor to fill a skills shortage. The skill must be unavailable in the U.S. and essential to the success of the business. Essential does not necessarily mean complicated. Marine products technicians hold essential skills due to a U.S. skills shortage, not because of the complexity of processing fish.

- The drawback to the E essential skill category is that you must agree to train U.S. workers to eliminate the need for an essential skill employee. Because of the training requirements, it's difficult to convince consuls to renew E essential skill visas. Although you can claim high turnover, or changes in technology prevented you from training a replacement, there is a limit to the consul's patience.

- The more esoteric or complicated the skill the easier the case. For example, it's easier to convince consuls or the INS that a nuclear physicist working on a new atom-smasher holds more essential skills or specialized knowledge than a noodle technician. In the case of the nuclear physicist, emphasize the complexity of the skill. In the case of the noodle technician, emphasize the contribution to local employment and the export trade.

- Time Limits: Consuls issue E visas for up to five years. E visas may be renewed as long as you can convince the consul to issue the visa. There is no limit on extensions. The law limits L-1B visa validity to a total of five continuous years. After the five-year period, the applicant must leave the U.S. for a year before applying again.

The "Technicians" Option

If the applicant fails to qualify for any other nonimmigrant status, consider the H-2B visa, which applies to labor—skilled or unskilled—unavailable in the area of intended employment. The key factor here is availability. It does not matter whether you import rocket scientists or ditch diggers as long as the labor is unavailable.

H-2B workers must work seasonally or fill a one-time need. Trainers coming to the U.S. to teach American workers a procedure, such as a chef showing American cooks a new cuisine, fill a one-time need. Theoretically, the trainee takes over the position. This does not apply to child monitors or amahs, who fill a nonrecurring position. The child eventually grows up.

The employer must advertise the position, interview the job applicants, and convince the Department of Labor that none of the job applicants meet the *minimum* job requirements. The Department of Labor establishes minimum job requirements and acceptable salaries, and determines which job applicants to interview. If you succeed with the Department of Labor, the job will be certified as available to foreign workers. Then you must petition the INS for visa approval.

The entire process takes between 90 and 120 days, and the H-2B visa lasts for one year. To extend the visa, the entire process must be repeated.

Recruitment Difficulties

If there is a choice, use the E-1 essential skill or L-1B specialized knowledge categories because they do not require recruitment. The recruitment process puts the employer in an awkward position. The employer hopes to prove that no qualified U.S. workers exist, and often does that by finding reasons not to hire the people answering the job advertisements. Understandably, the jilted job applicants often complain to the Department of Labor. The cost of advertising and inconvenience of interviewing undesirable applicants often make the process distasteful.

Other H-2B Applications

Use the H-2B visa when your employees fit into a category of workers who customarily use the H-2B visa, or there is no other choice. Sheep ranchers in Montana use H-2B visas for Basque shepherds. People who want to hire domestic help or someone to take care of their children use

H-2B visas for nannies and amahs. Restaurants sometimes use H-2B visas for chefs. Farmers use H-2A (agricultural) for farm workers. Manufacturers, when all else fails, use H-2B for technicians and trainers.

Marine Products Technicians

The marine products industry uses H-2B visas to send technicians to Alaska to process pollack, salmon, herring roe, surimi and other species of fish. The U.S. suffers a shortage of marine products technicians qualified to service foreign markets. Japanese, Korean and Norwegian companies send hundreds of marine products technicians to Alaska on a seasonal basis. The technicians work on short-term contracts. There is a long history of negotiation in this industry, with the INS and Department of Labor on one side and the marine products industry in opposition.

The U.S. packer wants to ensure that the product meets buyer's specifications before it reaches the market. The buyer who distributes the products abroad wants assurance that the product meets his market requirements. To meet contractual requirements, the buyer must send its technicians to each packing plant to render technical assistance and quality control. This is a perfect scenario for using H-2B visas.

Since there is no American market for most of the marine products exported to Japan, few qualified U.S. workers exist. And since foreign technicians only work on short-term contracts, there is no sense applying for long-term visas, such as E-1 essential skill or L-1B specialized knowledge. Employers may spread advertising and recruitment over many visas, as up to 50 technicians often apply at the same time. Advertising and recruitment costs can be prohibitive when applications are made for only a few technicians at a time. Finally, because of its long history of negotiation, the Department of Labor understands the need for foreign technicians and, to an extent, cooperates with the industry.

Review of Guidelines for Specialists

- All things being equal, use L-1B or E essential skills as opposed to H-2B.

- Use E essential skill or L-1B specialized knowledge for long-term technician employees. If an employee only works on a short-term basis, consider the H-2B category.

- Choosing between L-1B or E essential skill visas usually hinges on whether you feel the INS or a consul is more receptive to supporting your situation.

- Always apply for the maximum number of H-2B positions. You may have to hire U.S. workers. You want to make sure U.S. workers can be hired while still bringing in your minimum requirement of foreign employees.

- To show good faith in recruiting American workers, provide the Department of Labor with plans to eliminate dependence on foreign workers.

- Remember, cooperate with the Department of Labor during the H-2B process, and don't get frustrated.

Rectifying the "Foreign" Image

The U.S. subsidiary or branch office of a foreign company often employs more alien workers than Americans. Many companies prefer to use their own employees to make large purchases, handle money, or ensure quality control.

These factors combine to limit the number of American workers above the secretarial level in the U.S. operation.

Consulates often notice the high ratio of foreign professional workers and strongly suggest hiring more local employees. For immigration purposes, green card holders are U.S. workers. Many companies solve the consular-imposed problem by obtaining green cards for managerial staff.

Wage & Promotional Discrimination

U.S. workers must be paid the same salary as the foreign worker for the same work. Foreign transferees are often compensated for their overseas work by receiving bonuses paid from abroad as well as enhanced company benefits and housing allowances.

When evaluating the wage discrimination issue, pay close attention to the respective compensation and promotional packages offered to foreign and American workers. If the foreign worker receives a higher compensation package than the U.S. worker for the same work, be prepared to face a lawsuit. Also expect litigation if the U.S. employee does not progress through the company ranks at the same rate as the equally qualified foreign worker. The federal Equal Employment Opportunity Commission often supports such lawsuits in order to uphold anti-discrimination laws.

Branch offices worry less about these types of concerns. Most FCN and BIT treaties, in so many words, give branch offices the right to discriminate in favor of treaty nationals holding E-1 or E-2 visas. There is no right to discriminate in favor of H and L visa holders working for a treaty company. The U.S. Supreme Court made that decision and it's still the law, though it is currently under attack. Given the correct facts, this exception to the civil rights laws may change. This is one of the few advantages of operating as a branch office.

The law requires all employers to provide equal pay for equal work. Equal pay for equal work means general equality of the net result, not identical benefit and compensation packages. Equal pay for equal work, full disclosure of job duties and compensation packages, as well as general fairness will solve most problems between foreign and local staffmembers.

Chapter 8

Five Ways to Obtain a "Green Card"

Foreign companies usually move
employees to America in order to staff
a business. Foreign nationals, most often,
establish a U.S. business as a vehicle for
permanently moving their families to the U.S.
Among the more common reasons for
moving to the U.S. are concerns for safety,
fear of instability or unpredictability
with the home country's government,
children's schooling, quality of life,
and retirement.

Investors who merely wish to invest or own property in the U.S. needn't read any more of this chapter. Anyone can buy property, open a bank account, operate a business, or own a house in the U.S. without a visa. Some nations—not the U.S.—permit self-supporting people to retire or reside indefinitely in their country. People who wish to live, work or retire in the U.S. require a visa.

Moving to a strange country involves planning and patience, and most people require several years to make the transition of living comfortably in the U.S. People commonly work in the home country during the transition period, while the children or family members live in America. Everyone who decides to move to America must resolve unique problems. Yet the goal of permanent U.S. residence remains the same. Several visa strategies may accomplish this same result:

- Family Class: Application through a close family member.
- Investment in the U.S.
- Application on the basis of extraordinary skills.
- The Two-Step: Managerial transfer.
- Labor Certification: U.S. employer proves that no U.S. workers can fill your job.

General Concepts

The "green card" is evidence of Lawful Permanent Residence status. The credit card-sized green card is officially called an Alien Registration Card. The card was originally green, but was subsequently changed to blue, then pink. Despite the changes in color the green card retained its original name.

Any green card application requires three basic steps. Unless exempted, all employee-based permanent residence applicants must first prove that no American citizens meet the minimum job requirements ("labor certification"). We discuss the following exemptions: exceptional skills, national interest waiver, investment or employment creation, and multinational manager. Family-class green card applicants do not need labor certification. Secondly, the applicant must file an immigrant visa petition with the INS on the prescribed form. Finally, upon petition approval the applicant must file documents for the green card interview.

The Petition

The green card petition requests classification as a particular category of permanent resident. Family-class applicants use Form-I-130, employment class applicants use Form I-140, and investors use Form I-526. The petition and supporting documents are filed at an INS Regional Processing Center. The applicant then must wait for the result. The INS will either issue an approval letter, deny the application, or ask for more information. The processing period is about 90 days. Upon petition approval, assuming a visa is available, applicants may proceed to the next step, the interview.

The Quota

In order to interview, the INS must approve the petition and a visa must be available. Petitioners often encounter a waiting period. This "Quota Wait" occurs between the petition filing date and the date a visa becomes available.

The U.S. quota system seeks to limit annual permanent residence visas to approximately 480,000 family class,

140,000 employment class, 10,000 special immigrants (such as investors), and 55,000 diversity class (called lottery) divided among the various permanent residence categories. The quota exempts immediate relatives, spouses, parents and children of U.S. citizens who may interview immediately after visa approval.

The visa allocation formula annually grants each country or group of countries approximately 25,000 visas. Quota waits occur when a country uses its annual visa allotments plus unused visas from other countries. For example, high demand from countries such as Korea, China, India and Mexico has caused a minimum nine-year quota wait for brothers and sisters of U.S. citizens of these origins. On the other hand, most employment-based categories experience no quota wait.

The waiting period begins on the date (called the "priority date") of filing the petition with the INS or Department of Labor, as the case may be. Persons holding a current priority date may file for the interview. The State Department publishes "The Visa Bulletin," which lists current priority dates by category once a month. Because visa demand varies by country and visa category, there is no way to accurately predict the movement of priority dates.

Green Card Interview

The interview verifies eligibility for an immigration classification, and checks for grounds of exclusion from the U.S. Grounds for exclusion include criminal records, undesirable political affiliations, certain diseases, and lack of financial support. You may interview with the INS at an office nearest your U.S. residence, or you may interview with the U.S. Consulate nearest your place of foreign residence. The INS process is called an Adjustment of Status to Permanent Residence. The consular process is called Application for Immigrant Visa and Alien Registration. Both processes achieve the same ultimate results.

The term "Adjust Status to Permanent Residence" refers to the procedures required to change from a nonimmigrant or illegal status to a permanent resident. Until recently, no alien—except for immediate relatives—could interview in the U.S. without being of legal status. Now, aliens in illegal status may Adjust to Permanent Residence simply by paying five times the normal filing fee.

The INS and consulates require the same basic information and tend to ask the same interview questions. In choosing whether to interview with the INS or a consulate, consider local processing times, local enforcement policies and convenience, which vary among INS offices and consular posts.

People fearing strict consular enforcement often choose to interview with the INS. If problems arise, they may remain in the U.S. while solving the problem. If problems occur during a consular interview, one usually must remain abroad until they are resolved. Also, appeals of an INS decision can be made to an independent court. If a consul denies an application, the matter must be resolved with the U.S. State Department. No independent judges review consular decisions.

Green card petitions include spouses and children under age 21, as of the approval date of the adjustment of status or consular application. For example, your child turns 21 on March 1, 1995 and you filed the adjustment of status documents on December 1, 1994. If the INS approves the adjustment of status to permanent residence on March 2, 1995, the 21-year-old child will not qualify.

Children over 21 are eligible for second-family preference. Due to the quota wait, now approximately two years, the child must obtain another visa status through employment or as a student to remain in the U.S.

Exclusion

If the interviewing officer finds grounds for exclusion, you may apply for a waiver of the exclusion. The INS routinely grants waivers to Chinese or Russians who were members of the Communist Party, as well as for aliens with medical problems. It rarely waives drug offenses.

Green Card Categories

Let's examine the various approaches to obtaining a green card, and explore the easiest options first.

Pursue the Easiest Method First — Family Class

Family class petitions require proof of a qualifying relationship. Qualifying relationships include:

- Immediate Relative: Parents and spouses of U.S. citizens

- 1st Preference: Unmarried children of U.S. citizens

- 2nd Preference: Spouses and unmarried children of permanent residents (unmarried children under 21 [2A] have priority over unmarried children over 21 [2B])

- 3rd Preference: Married children of U.S. citizens

- 4th Preference: Brothers and sisters of adult U.S. citizens.

"Family Class" merely requires proof of the qualifying family relationship. Most people do not use lawyers for family class cases, except for convenience or in the case of missing or nonexistent records. In most cases, if you can't prove that your mother is your mother, there is a problem no lawyer can solve. You may want to consult with an expert to guide you through the filing and interview procedures, help you organize important evidence, and assist with timing.

NOTE: More than likely, Congress will eliminate the brother-sister and the adult children over 21 categories. There will be clean-up provisions for previously filed cases. The elimination of these categories will create more demand for employment- or investment-related visa categories.

The Petition

The petition (Form I-130) generally requires proof of the U.S. status of a relative and proof of relationship with that relative. To prove the required family relationship, attach the applicant's and sponsor's birth certificates, and provide proof of the sponsor's U.S. citizenship or permanent resident status. The instructions on the I-130 Form suggest appropriate supporting documents and explain the filing procedures.

Planning for the Quota Waiting Period

The quota waiting period— the period beginning after visa approval and ending with visa availability—presents the biggest obstacle in family class cases, since it may cause several years of separation from family members. Adult siblings of U.S. citizens usually work or manage businesses during the waiting period. Spouses and parents of American citizens experience no quota wait. The most common problem concerns spouses and children of green card holders.

A typical scenario: A husband with a green card marries a foreigner. The husband files for a green card and the INS approves a second preference petition for the new wife. A two-year quota wait is projected. The wife has no visa status other than a tourist visa.

What does this couple do during the quota waiting period? If the wife wants to live in the U.S. with her husband, rather than merely visiting him, she will need independent visa status. Two choices should be examined here. The wife may find a job that leads to an independent visa, such as H-1B or E, or attend school on an F-1 visa. If neither of these visas can be arranged, the wife can only have short-term visits with her husband.

Depending on nationality, one may visit the U.S. on visa waiver or with a B-2 tourist visa. Since visa waiver limits the visit to 90 days with no extensions, most spouses prefer a B-2 visa. As a rule, consuls do not issue B-2 visas to foreign spouses coming to the U.S. to visit their American mates. If possible, apply for the B-2 visa before marrying.

Negotiating the Waiting Period with a B-2 Visa

Most B-2 visas allow multiple entries over a five-year period. The INS usually admits B-2 visa holders for six months, and it's relatively easy to extend for an additional six months. But subsequent extensions are difficult. Plan on returning home after the one-year period. The second preference waiting period—for spouses of green card holders—is approximately two years. The B-2 visa method usually covers one of the two years.

Aliens cannot come to the U.S. on a temporary visa when they intend to live permanently in the country. The INS generally assumes that a wife coming to visit her husband—or vice versa—intends to live with the spouse. The chances of entering the U.S. may depend upon convincing an INS inspector that the visit is truly temporary.

It is easier to demonstrate intentions for *temporary* visits to the U.S. if you have a job, family and property in your home country. For obvious reasons, the longer you stay home between trips the more clear it is that there are meaningful ties to your home country. Factors which prove an intention to return home after a short visit include a job or business in the home country, a residence, family, and proof that you've returned home after previous U.S. visits.

Be honest, prepare supporting evidence, and make sure the INS appreciates the applicant's knowledge and understanding of the rules. If there is a choice, enter on a B-2 rather than on visa waiver. With a B-2, the INS cannot refuse entry, especially if a hearing is requested. With a visa waiver, there is no right to a hearing and one can be sent home immediately.

If the applicant told the truth and has ample supporting documentation, the solution is to request a hearing when denied entry. In most cases, the INS will grant admittance rather than schedule a hearing. In the worst cases, one might spend a night or two in immigration jail before your spouse can arrange bail. A loving spouse is worth it!

Negotiating the Quota Waiting Period by Finding a Job

Holders of university degrees may seek a sponsoring employer and explore the filing of an H-1B petition. If the spouse finds an employer of the same nationality qualified for E visa status, consider an E visa. Visa waiver or B-2 visa holders may legally look for jobs in the U.S. B-2 visa holders may find a job and change status in the U.S.

Many people change from B-2 to H-1B or E visa status and wait in the U.S., without leaving, until the green card is available. Since visa waiver holders may not change to another nonimmigrant status in the U.S. after finding employment, they must obtain INS approval and return home to apply for the visa. All nonimmigrant visa applicants must disclose the green card applications submitted on their behalf. The INS cannot deny nonimmigrant work visa petitions solely because of a pending green card application.

Negotiating the Quota Waiting Period As a Student

Some spouses go to school as F-1 students. This option works for those who intend to go to school or want to continue school but need a compelling reason to do so. Only serious students need apply, as a full course load must be maintained in order to keep the F-1 visa.

In Sum...

If the quota waiting period separates a foreign family member from a U.S. relative, there are four choices: Waiting at home, visiting the U.S., finding an American job, and changing to a nonimmigrant work visa. Or, go to school and change to F-1 status. In all cases, one must be able to prove intention to return home at the end of the temporary stay, in spite of a pending green card petition.

For the Wealthy — An "Investor Program"

The U.S., like Canada, Australia, New Zealand and other countries, has an immigrant investor program. The U.S. requires an investment of $1,000,000 in a trade or business, and employment of 10 full-time persons. The American program is officially called the Employment Creation Aliens Program, or more commonly, the Investor Visa. The program reduces the investment amount to $500,000 for rural or high-unemployment areas.

The U.S. program began in 1990. One of our first immigrant investor cases involved a mother and her two daughters, each of whom purchased 16.66 percent of a construction company and large shopping mall. The husband had given the mother and each daughter $1,000,000, for a total of $3,000,000, in a divorce settlement. The funds came from a U.S. bank account. Although the mother and daughters served on the company's board of directors, they had no active roles in management. The project employed about 45 people, some on a part-time basis. This case satisfied the regulatory requirements and was duly approved.

NOTE: It is possible that, through future legislation, Congress may eliminate the $500,000 investment level and make $1,000,000 the minimum investment.

Employee Criteria

Any trade or business that employs at least 10 persons per investor qualifies for this program. One may start a business, buy a business, or invest in an existing commercial concern. The investment must increase the capital or employment of an existing business by at least 140 percent. The people in the example above invested in an existing business.

Immigrant investors may hold minority interests in the business. Although investors must play a role in management, the regulations deem limited partners or members of the board of directors as active participants in management. As long as the business employs at least 10 persons per investor, it may accept as many investors who make the required investment.

A "full-time employee" is defined as someone working at least 37.5 hours per week. But employers may combine part-time employees to satisfy the definition. Twenty people who work 18.75 hours each equals 10 employees. Independent contractors, such as tradespeople and cleaning service personnel, do not count as employees. Employees may not be immediate family members of the investor, but must be U.S. citizens or green card holders.

Investment Fund Sources

Investment funds may come from any legal foreign or U.S. source, including gifts and divorce settlements. Corporate investors may not designate an employee or shareholder to receive the green card. Whoever receives the visa must make the investment. Borrowed investment funds qualify as long as the borrowed funds are not secured by the assets of the target U.S. business. For example, investors may borrow against a home and use the loan proceeds to buy a business qualifying for the investor visa.

Business Plan

The INS application, Form I-526, must include a business plan which demonstrates that the target business will support at least 10 employees. It must also show proof of the required capital. Investors have two years to make the investment and hire 10 employees. The INS grants a conditional green card upon the initial investment, and two years later issues an unrestricted green card upon verification of the required employees and capital. There is no requirement to continue the investment beyond the two-year period.

The "Regional Center" Program

The 10-employee requirement deters most investors. To encourage immigrant investors, the INS, in 1994, devised a slightly different scheme. Now, immigrant investors may invest in INS-approved funds called "Regional Centers." The regional centers are any project—private or public—that promotes U.S. employment and exports in a particular region of the U.S.

In this program the promoter makes a proposal to the INS in Washington D.C. If the INS believes the proposal will benefit a regional economy and shows potential for providing significant employment opportunities, the project will be designated a regional center. With INS approval in hand, the promoter forms a limited partnership or corporation to raise money. Foreign investors may apply for green cards upon making the investment.

Investors in a regional center do not have to prove the business will employ 10 persons. Instead, the regional center may rely on government or private industry job multiplier statistics to prove required employment. For example, a regional center proposing to develop an air cargo facility may rely on the indirect employment created by the air cargo facility to satisfy the 10-employee requirement. Indirect employment includes direct employment plus jobs such as service industries that rely on the regional center. If the job multiplier statistics demonstrate the regional center will create 500 direct and indirect jobs, the regional center may seek 50 investors. Most state economic development agencies provide job multiplier statistics.

Except for employment creation, regional centers must follow the same rules as those for the immigrant investor program in the employment creation criteria.

Some Pitfalls with Regional Center Investments

The regional center program permits those who have money, but do not want to manage a U.S. business and hire U.S. workers, to obtain green cards. Shop carefully and investigate the management team. Look for an exit strategy. How does management intend to repay investors? For example, a regional center owning real estate may intend to refinance property to repay investors. It's easier to refinance buildings than to refinance or sell a business.

A regional center investment is, in theory, no different than a syndicated fund except that participants receive a green card. Regional center investors take the risk of placing money in the hands of the regional center manager. The regional center may fail within the two-year conditional green card period, and investors could lose their money and green cards. The INS has no plan to deal with this unfortunate possibility.

Who Manages Regional Centers?

Individuals, corporations and government agencies are eligible to manage regional center projects. Local governments were responsible for sponsoring two of the first seven funds. Our law firm has established several privately-managed funds. Since government can also mismanage money, don't be comforted by its sponsorship of a fund.

For obvious reasons, very few people utilized the regional center or immigrant investor program at the $1,000,000 level. Regional centers located in rural or high-unemployment areas, i.e. the $500,000 investments, are becoming popular in many Asian countries. Agents located in Taiwan, Hong Kong and Japan offer a variety of regional center investment opportunities. We carefully monitor regional center activity, but because of rapid changes we did not publish activity lists in this book.

Retirement in America — "The Two-Step" Method For Managers & Executives

As the fastest and easiest method for businesspeople to obtain green cards, the Two-Step Method permits international managers and executives to apply for green cards without labor certification. The exemption from labor certification saves considerable time and expense. The Two-Step works for managerial/executive transferees working for established international organizations, as well as those who create an international organization and transfer themselves to manage the U.S. operation.

Step 1 refers to transferring in a managerial capacity to the U.S. within an international organization. This requires establishing a U.S. business qualifying as an L-1 international organization, or using an existing L-1 international organization and obtaining a nonimmigrant work visa as a managerial transfer.

The applicant must have worked in a managerial or executive capacity on the foreign side of the international organization for one of the three years prior to the transfer to the U.S. branch, subsidiary or affiliate of the foreign employer in a managerial or executive capacity.

Step 2 refers to the green card procedures, which may occur at any time after the U.S. employer has been doing business for one year.

The Two-Step applies to international managers and executives regardless of visa type. Therefore, managers and executives may use H-1A, E-1/2 or H-1B visas. The exemption from labor certification focuses on transfer in a managerial capacity within an international organization, not the particular visa used to effect the transfer.

A Common Scenario

Let's look at how the Two-Step might work for an individual. A "Mr. Smith" owns an electric motor parts trading company in a foreign country. He wants his children to receive an American education, and his wife wants to live in the U.S. with the children while they attend school. The Smiths ultimately want to retire in the U.S., so Mr. Smith needs a long-term visa strategy for the entire family.

The First Step

Mr. Smith establishes a U.S. subsidiary company and secures an office. He then applies for an L-1A visa to manage the new American company during the start-up phase. Smith's wife and children receive L-2 visas as dependents, thus allowing them to attend school. Mrs. Smith may live with the children, but is not allowed to work. The L-1A must be extended after the first year. Managers of start-up companies must establish the company within one year. Mr. Smith applies for and receives a two-year extension.

The Second Step

Immediately after the extension approval, Mr. Smith applies for a green card as an "International Manager or Executive." Upon green card approval, he submits documents for the family's interview. If all goes well, Mr. Smith receives a temporary green card within eight to 12 months of his petition, and he'll receive a permanent green card about four months later. Within two years after arriving in America, Mr. Smith, his wife and their children under 21 years of age will have green cards.

If Mr. Smith works for an established company, he may immediately apply for a green card. The exemption from labor certification depends upon managerial/executive transfer within an international organization that has been doing business in the U.S. for at least one year. The applicant needn't work in the U.S. for one year. Theoretically, the applicant could apply from abroad as long as the international organization conducted business in the U.S. for one year as the one-year period refers to the employer, not the applicant.

Details of the Two-Step Process

Step 1. Establish the U.S. Business/Managerial Transfer with a Nonimmigrant Work Visa

Establishing a U.S. Subsidiary

Establishing a company means incorporating a business, obtaining federal tax identification numbers, finding a place of business, and getting relevant licenses. For a variety of tax and legal reasons, we recommend establishing a U.S. corporation rather than a U.S. branch office. In most cases, the applicant should issue shares to the foreign employer, which becomes the parent company. The subsidiary company must either lease or buy a place of doing business. Do not operate from a personal residence because the INS will query it.

The U.S. company may buy property, purchase a business, or start a new firm. Conduct any business as long as it requires the services of a manager or executive. As a general rule, the business must hire employees; a one-person operation does not require a manager. The business plan should require at least three or four employees.

88

Any business qualifies for the Two-Step—real estate investor, import/export trader, merchant, manufacturer, restaurant manager or manager of a group of professionals. In fact, the U.S. trade or business may be unrelated to the foreign parent's line of business. The foreign parent could be a trading company, while the U.S. subsidiary could be a real estate management firm.

Choosing a Nonimmigrant Work Visa

For green card purposes, any nonimmigrant work visa suffices as long as one transfers to the U.S. branch, subsidiary or affiliate of the foreign employer in a managerial capacity. Established companies generally use the L-1A or E-1/2 options. Although H-1B visa holders may also serve in a managerial capacity, we don't recommend using H-1B status as a stepping stone in the Two-Step process. Consider the time and effort required to convince the INS that the H-1B professional also serves in a managerial position. The INS would want a convincing explanation as to why a managerial visa was not used in the first place. Most start-up companies should use the L-1A visa. Examine all visa options. Just make sure to transfer to the U.S. as a manager.

Factors such as the nature of the U.S. business, nationality, convenience and consular vs. INS enforcement policies determines whether application should be made for E-1, E-2 or L-1A status. The INS will grant an initial one-year validity period for L-1A start-up companies. At the end of the one-year period, the INS requires proof of progress toward establishing the U.S. business. Consuls often deny E visa status for start-up companies.

E or L managers may be paid from the foreign parent

company and commute between the U.S. office and overseas location. Two-Step managers may work part-time in the U.S. However, Two-Step managers must prove they exercise managerial control over the U.S. business. Proof of managerial control includes authority to sign company documents, a history of reviewing company operations, management memoranda, minutes of management decisions, contract negotiation, hiring and firing, and budgetary authority.

Step 2. One Year of Doing Business, Multinational Manager Green Card

Apply for the green card as a first preference multinational manager anytime after the U.S. company has been doing business in the U.S. for one year. "Doing business" means regularly and systematically providing goods and services to customers. The INS verifies gross sales, employment and business activity. Remember that most managers must hire subordinate employees to prove service in a managerial capacity. Persons managing a function or a division of a large company, i.e. a regional sales manager, do not need subordinate employees. This exception to the employee requirement does not help many small business applicants.

The "one year of doing business" requirement means that the company did business in the U.S. for a year. It does not mean that the individual, the transferee, worked in the U.S. for a year. In other words, the applicant's foreign company can buy an established U.S. business with a multi-year operating history. Since the U.S. business operated for over one year, it means immediate transfer of the person to the new U.S. subsidiary as a first preference multinational manager, skipping the first step of the Two-Step.

Another Two-Step Approach:
Green Cards for Corporate Executives or Managers & Established Organizations

Corporate executives and managers for established international organizations use the same Two-Step process as individual businessmen, but they benefit from a ready-made international organization. Individual businesspeople must create their own international organization.

As a rule, an employer transfers a manager to a U.S. member of the international organization using an L-1 or E-1/2 visa. In the typical situation, the manager worked in a managerial capacity for a member of the international organization for one of the three years prior to being transferred to the U.S. The American operation has been doing business for more than one year prior to the transfer. This type of manager may apply for a green card immediately upon arrival in the U.S. Theoretically, the manager could apply for a green card before transfer while working for the parent company abroad.

Benefits for Children & Retirement

Many people seek green cards because their children want to attend an American university or they plan to retire in the U.S. Dependent children need a separate visa to remain in the U.S. after the age of 21, usually F-1 student or a nonimmigrant work visa. At retirement, an executive or manager will no longer be an employee of an international organization. Upon retirement, he must apply for a green card through investment, skills or family-ties types of petitions. It's easier to obtain a green card as a multinational manager because of the exemption from labor certification.

Children under age 21 may simultaneously obtain green

cards through parents as well as find a job after graduation without having to apply for a work visa. As a permanent U.S. resident, the child may qualify for lower-cost resident tuition at state universities (private universities usually charge the same expensive tuition to all students). The savings in state university tuition for one child more than pays for any immigration legal fees, and is one of the better investments you can make.

Employer's Point of View

Many employers resist green card applications of employees since green card holders may work anywhere they choose. After all, why go through the time and expense of a green card application only to lose an employee? Conversely, nonimmigrant visa holders must work for the sponsoring employer.

Most middle-aged green card applicants worked their entire careers for a single corporate group, and it is difficult to find an equivalent job in the U.S. Very few people want to move to a new company in a foreign land at the middle or end of their careers. Most want to spend more time on the golf course or in other leisure activities rather than undergo a midlife career change. Those new to the corporate group pose a greater risk of using the employer to obtain a green card and then leaving.

Foreign-owned U.S. employers may benefit when an executive or manager obtains a green card. Employers must file an Embassy Annual Report for E visa purposes, listing U.S. and foreign workers and their positions. The embassy uses this report to monitor how many E visas it will grant for particular positions. Green card holders count as American workers and may free up a new E visa position.

Timing & Procedure

Nonimmigrant Work Visa (Step 1)

File L-1A petitions at an INS regional center. File E visa petitions at a consular or regional center. INS filings require Form 129 and an L or E Supplement. Each consulate uses its own forms. Expect L-1A or E-1/2 visa processing to take 90 days. E visa processing times depend upon a particular consulate's policies. Unless buying or working for an existing business, one must wait until the U.S. business can prove one year of active operation before applying for the green card. In Two-Step cases, the green card application contains much of the same information as the L-1A or E visa petition.

Green Card (Step 2)

File Form I-140 (Petition for Immigrant Worker) and supporting documents with the INS at a Regional Service Center. Allow 90 days for regional center processing. Upon petition approval, file for a green card interview with the INS or consulate. Currently, multinational managers endure no quota waiting period.

The Green Card Interview

INS Interview

Most Two-Step applicants interview with the INS because their families already live in the U.S. Choose whether to interview with the INS or a consulate on the I-140 petition. To interview in the U.S., file the Adjustment of Status Package (Form I-485) and supporting documents with the INS. Most INS offices only conduct personal interviews for suspicious business-class cases. Otherwise, the INS merely reviews the adjustment of status documents, verifies police records, and usually mails the result and, hopefully, a temporary green card four to six months after the filing. The temporary green card should be followed by the permanent green card within four months. Adjustment procedures vary among the INS district offices.

Consular Interview

Alternatively, one may interview at a consulate. In the case of consular interviews, the INS sends files to a visa distribution center in New Hampshire, called the National Visa Center (NVC). The NVC sends a biographical information package (called "Packet 3") to the applicant and forwards the file to the correct consular post. The consulate contacts the applicant with interview details. Interview procedures vary among consular offices. Applicants generally receive a temporary green card at the time of the consular interview.

The Green Card

The temporary green card, usually valid for six months, serves as a travel document and confers the same benefits as the permanent green card. The INS routinely extends temporary green cards if receipt of the permanent green card is delayed. Most interviewing INS offices issue the temporary green card on a letter-sized page or as an endorsed I-94 card. The permanent green card, a plastic card manufactured in Arlington, Texas, contains the recipient's picture, fingerprint, date of birth, date of approval and other details.

Separate Interviews for Family Members

Green card approval includes spouses and children under 21. Circumstances often cause families to be interviewed in different places. The principal alien—the one who received green card approval—must interview first and obtain approval either at a consular post or INS office. The applicant must instruct the interviewing office to send the approval notice and file to wherever the rest of the family will interview. The receiving post will notify the family of the interview dates. These procedures (called "Following to Join") delay the process, and there is a risk of losing the file during transfer between interviewing offices.

Travel During the INS Interview Process

Two-Step businesspersons often make frequent trips abroad. The nonimmigrant visa automatically expires upon filing for adjustment of status with the INS, which means that adjustment applicants have no travel document between the date of the filing the adjustment petition with the INS and receipt of the temporary green card. Therefore, one needs "Advance Parole" to travel abroad and return to the U.S. Advance Parole serves as a travel document to enable travel abroad between the date of the filing adjustment of status forms with the INS and receipt of the temporary green card. The INS grants advance parole for business reasons or family emergencies. But note that procedures vary among INS offices. Those who interview before a consul need not worry about travel arrangements since, in most cases, the nonimmigrant visa usually remains valid until the interview date and receipt of the temporary green card.

The INS assumes those who travel without advance parole have abandoned their adjustment of status petition. Offenders must either start over or interview at an overseas consulate. Unfortunately, the INS enforces this nonsensical rule. It's much better to apply for advance parole than fight the system.

Common Pitfalls

The lack of a foreign parent company destroys the required international organization. Multinational managers must belong to an international organization until receipt of the green card. So don't sell or close the foreign parent company after establishing a U.S. subsidiary. If necessary, close the company after receiving the green card.

The Two-Step works because it qualifies for an exemption to labor certification for managerial transfers within an international organization. Caution: The person who owns or manages a U.S. business as an individual rather than through an international organization is ineligible for the exemption from labor certification.

Labor certification requires the employer to prove that no U.S. workers meet the job's minimum requirements. If no qualified U.S. workers apply, the U.S. Department of Labor (DOL) will certify the position as available to foreign workers. This process may take up to two years.

To make matters worse, the DOL will not certify self-employed people because it assumes the self-employed worker will refuse to make their job available to U.S. workers. (What business owner will fire himself when a qualified U.S. worker appears?) Self-employed people who are not multinational managers cannot use the Two-Step process or obtain labor certification. Self-employed people should explore the investor visa, family class or exceptional skill categories.

Conclusion

At present, multinational managers experience no quota wait. Also, processing and procedural issues present few problems. Proposed cuts in employment-based immigration may create future quota waits. Prior to 1990 certain multinational managers experienced one- to two-year quota waits. Today is a good time to apply for a multinational manager green card. Indeed, the timing has never been better.

Those with Extraordinary Abilities in Sciences, Arts & Business

People recognized internationally at the top of their field qualify for this category. Celebrities, winners of Nobel Prizes, or people with broad recognition qualify. Since the vast majority of readers will not qualify for this position, there is no need to elaborate on this type of visa petitioner beyond mention that it's available. Use forms I-140 and MA-750A and B for this category.

National Interest

Persons with exceptional ability in business and the arts or sciences, and whose skills serve American national interest, qualify for the "national interests" exemption from labor certification. A sponsoring employer is not necessary, and the petitioner may be self-employed. "Exceptional" means well above average but not extraordinary, as in "Extraordinary Ability." Though the INS only vaguely defines the term "national interest," the lack of detail creates an opportunity. Rather than restricting the category to, say, scientists with doctoral degrees or engineers, the INS invites the applicant to make a proposal.

The INS focuses on whether the applicant's skills serve

America's national interests. Although most cases involve aliens with advanced education, patents or other obvious qualifications (such as participation in important projects), there are enough exceptions to recommend this category to anyone who feels their skills contribute to the artistic, economic, business or scientific interests of the U.S.

As an example of the program's flexibility, a salmon aquaculturist with no formal training was qualified under this petition. We argued that salmon farming is necessary in the face of declining natural salmon runs. Persons with unique knowledge of foreign markets often qualify. Businessmen with records for turning companies around may also qualify. (Interestingly, the INS holds that attorneys do not qualify for this category.)

This category may be used in tandem with labor certification. Prospective employers should apply for this category, and simultaneously start the labor certification process. If the INS approves the national-interest petition, stop the labor certification process. If the petition is denied, continue with labor certification. The INS usually responds before one is committed beyond the point of no return in the labor certification process. Remember, labor certification is the last resort, and happiness is found when cancelling that application. Use forms I-140 and MA-750A and B for this category.

NOTE: Congress may impose a revised labor certification system. Instead of recruitment, the employer would promise to pay the alien 110% of the prevailing wage, plus pay a fee equal to 30% of the first-year's salary to the DOL to be used for training U.S. workers. There is a small chance that this or a similar provision will become law. Congress will most certainly establish minimum experience requirements for extraordinary ability, national interest waiver, or outstanding researchers. The most likely scenario will require the applicant to prove five years of job-related experience outside of the U.S.

The Last Resort: Labor Certification

Those who don't qualify for an exemption from labor certification, read this section.

General

The applicant for labor certification must have an employer willing to advertise the position and prove to the DOL that no U.S. worker meets the minimum job requirements. Quite often, after interviewing countless applicants—all with credentials similar to a foreign application, the DOL determines that the foreigner is the only one who qualifies. The labor certification system tries to ensure jobs for U.S. workers who can meet minimum job requirements.

An employer should be aware that this process may take up to a year to complete. But the wait is worth it. Legal fees and the costs of advertising and other items range from $5,000 to $10,000 for the entire process, which includes labor certification, green card petition and interview.

In a typical case the applicant works for the prospective employer on an H-1B visa. Remember, H-1B visa holders generally don't qualify for the Two-Step. The U.S. employer is pleased with the applicant's work and will go through the labor certification process to keep the employee. There is no requirement to work for the prospective U.S. employer during the labor certification process; one may work abroad while the American employer files for labor certification of the individual.

The DOL administers the labor certification process. It contracts with individual state job services or state departments of labor to conduct local labor recruitment and manage communications with the employer. The state job service recommends approval or disapproval to the DOL.

Job Requirements & Prevailing Wage

Labor certification means that the DOL has determined no available U.S. workers meet the minimum job requirements. Upon receipt of labor certification, the applicant may petition for a visa through the INS. Every employment-based green card applicant must go through labor certification unless they qualify for one of the exemptions previously discussed.

The employer must prove that no American workers meet the minimum job requirements at the prevailing wage. The DOL determines the minimum job requirements and prevailing wage. The employer must advertise for and try to recruit persons meeting the minimum requirements, not the most qualified persons as in a normal situation.

The salary offered to the alien must equal or exceed the prevailing wage. The prevailing wage, based on DOL surveys, reflects the wage commonly paid for similar positions in the area of intended employment. Since most employers won't hire the worst person for the job, the prevailing wage actually represents the wage employers expect to pay to the person most suitable for the job.

The labor certification process forces employers to advertise for a person who meets the minimum job requirements, while offering the wages paid to the most qualified applicants. In a normal situation, employers hire the best person for the least money, not the worst person at the salary paid to the best people. Despite the bizarre logic of this process, most labor certification petitions are successful.

Labor Certification Forms

The labor certification form, ETA 750A, describes the job offer for recruitment purposes. It contains fill-in blocks for the General Job Description (Block 12), Education and Experience Requirements (Block 13), and Special Requirements (Block 14). ETA 750B contains blocks for the applicant's education and experience. Use this form to prove that the applicant meets the requirements of the job offered. There are different strategies for filling in the three key areas.

Steps in the Labor Certification Process

The labor certification process may be divided into five steps:

1. Creating the job description.
2. State employment service approval of the job description.
3. Recruitment and advertising.
4. Approval by the U.S. DOL.
5. Filing the Immigrant Visa petition with the INS.

Step 1. Creating the Job Description

The DOL recommends minimum job qualifications. These may include the required years of experience, education levels and specific job duties. Since the DOL bases job requirements on U.S. labor market surveys, American workers usually qualify for a job defined by the DOL. The DOL publishes the results of its surveys in the "Dictionary of Occupational Titles" and other manuals.

The onus is on the employer to convince the department that your position should include different job-related requirements than the department's standards. We generally start with the employer's actual job requirements. If the DOL objects, attempt to justify the employer's position based on the employer's past practices and business necessity. The idea is to convince the DOL that the employer based the job requirements on its normal hiring policies and did not tailor the job requirements to the applicant's skills and experience.

Sample Job Description—Block 12

The following might be used as a job description for the position of a marine products market researcher.

"Develop and maintain cost accounting system. Gather, compile and analyze information from various fish processing locations, unloading docks, freight companies, etc. Determine costs of finished fish products. Prepare entries to the general ledger accounts. Supervise and document the flow of finished products. Jointly prepare financial statements and perform financial analyses. Provide detailed monthly profit/loss information for each fish species and interpret the data to recommend improvement and support for managerial decisions. Responsibilities also include accounts payable functions, inventory control and other accounting tasks assigned by the accounting manager. All duties performed on computer. Conduct detailed market analysis of China/Taiwan market. Develop, negotiate, service Chinese accounts. Large portion of duties performed with LOTUS software."

Strategy

Provide as much detail as possible in a job description.

Divide the job into its smallest components, as each component becomes a job requirement. The more components the greater the chance that U.S. applicants will fail to meet a job requirement. Note the detail in the example cited.

All job requirements must have a relationship to performing the position. Be prepared to justify each job requirement. Ask yourself if you can perform the job without a particular requirement. If you can, the state Department of Labor, which reviews the job description, will strongly suggest elimination of that job requirement.

Education & Experience—Block 13

The following might be used as Education and Experience for the marine products market researcher position.

Education. A Bachelor of Arts degree in Accounting or Economics required for this position.

Experience Required. Job Experience - 3 Years; Related Occupation: None

Strategy

Employers who require more education and experience than suggested by the DOL must demonstrate the business necessity for the increased requirements. "Business necessity" means proving that the requirement is essential to the employer's business.

For example, an employer requiring a Masters degree in Accounting for a staff position and five years experience for an accountant must establish a business reason for requiring the Masters Degree, when most employers only require a Bachelor of Arts degree.

Because the Department of Labor bases educational and experience requirements on their job market surveys, it's difficult to deviate from their suggested requirements. Law courts tend to uphold the government job surveys. Without conducting your own job market survey, it's difficult to prove the inaccuracy of a DOL survey. On the other hand, the courts grant employers more latitude on the subject of actual job duties. For this reason it is preferred to argue about the job description and special requirements rather than the education and experience requirements.

A Trap: Experience Gained with the Petitioning Employer

The applicant cannot use job-related experience gained with the petitioning employer to qualify for the job. For example, a company providing household goods moving services to Japanese customers wishes to hire a household goods movements supervisor. The applicant worked in Japan for two years as a supervisor in a household goods moving company, and worked for the prospective U.S. employer for a year as a supervisor on an H-1B visa. The U.S. employer normally requires three years experience for supervisors.

The applicant has two years experience with another employer in Japan, and one year experience with the U.S. employer applying for the labor certification. The U.S. employer may only require two years experience as a supervisor, or it will exclude the applicant.

Special Requirements—Block 14

The following might be used in the Special Requirements block for the position of marine products market researcher.

Special Requirements. Minimum one year experience using LOTUS software system. Two years professional or business experience in China. Must read, write and speak fluent Mandarin Chinese. Experience may be gained concurrently. Resumé and two references required.

Strategy

The Special Requirements distinguish this job from similar jobs. These requirements should be tailored to the employer's business requirements, not the applicant's credentials. For example, all accountants keep books and prepare financial statements. The accountant in the example also uses a foreign accounting system and does business in a foreign language. Employers must justify all special requirements as a business necessity. "Business necessity" means that the requirement is essential to the employer's business success.

Justify language requirements by proving that the business must be conducted in the foreign language. For example, to prove that most of the customers speak Japanese, produce business correspondence and copies of phone bills. Use common sense to justify business necessity.

An accountant who audits both a U.S. subsidiary and the Chinese parent company must know both American and Chinese financial reporting systems. A company that recently acquired a foreign technology may require a person with experience in that technology. A company hoping to open a foreign market may need a person experienced in that market. A company providing services to foreign nationals in the U.S. may require the services of a person familiar with the particular customs and habits of the foreign nationals.

Step 2: State Job Service Processing

Once satisfied with the job description, the employer

must send it along with the application forms (ETA 750 A&B), a sample advertisement, and supporting documents proving the applicant's qualifications to the State Job Service. The advertisement recites the information contained in blocks 12, 13 and 14. The job service will normally assign a prevailing wage, assign a file number (called a "Job Order"), and ask the employer to justify some of the job requirements.

The employer may have to justify special requirements. For example, the employer may have to produce phone bills and correspondence to prove it does business in a foreign language. The job service may also question the years of experience or the level of education required. If the job offered combines aspects of two job descriptions, justify why the two job descriptions were combined in one position rather than simply hiring two people.

Most state job services are reasonable and, after some negotiations, will reach agreement on the content of the advertisement, job description, education and experience, and special requirements. State job service processing times vary by state; expect the process to take six months to a year.

Step 3: Recruitment

After reaching agreement on the content of the job description and other requirements, the state job service will suggest which periodicals or magazines to use for advertising the salary, job description and special requirements of the position. The advertisement must run for at least three days in a newspaper, usually including a Sunday, or one issue of a monthly magazine. Prospective applicants will send resumés to the job service or employer. The job services establish the recruiting procedures, then it advises the employer which applicants to be interviewed. The recruitment period lasts 30 days from the date the job service opens its job order.

Each interviewee must be notified (don't wait until the end of the recruitment period to contact applicants) by phone or letter, and be offered a personal interview. We recommend sending a registered letter to each applicant to show they were contacted. Employers must use normal interviewing policy, and each interviewee should be given written reasons for rejection. The reasons must relate to the job requirements.

Do not let a lawyer handle the interview. (How would you feel if you went to a job interview and faced a company lawyer?) The DOL feels the same way, and will deny the case because the interview process was unfair.

Step 4: Department of Labor Approval

After completing the recruitment process, the employer must prepare a written report detailing the results of each interview. The employer's report must show how each applicant failed to meet one or more of the job requirements. The employer sends the report to the job service, which will then recommend approval or denial to the U.S. Department of Labor. Since the DOL generally relies on the job service's recommendation, it's best to reach agreement with the job service on all important issues before advertising and recruitment. The DOL will advise the employer of its decision. Approval is called a Labor Certification. Labor Certification means that the DOL has certified the job as being available to foreign workers. You may appeal denials and, quite often, the DOL lets you provide additional information to support a case.

Step 5: INS Approval

With labor certification in hand, you may file the immigrant petition with the INS. Use the same Form I-140 as most other employment-based petitions. The filing and interview procedure is the same as for any other work-related immigrant visa petition. Generally, the INS approves cases with approved labor certifications. Occasionally, however, it will question an employer's ability to pay the salary of the new employee. In such cases, the employer must furnish tax returns and financial statements to prove it can afford to hire the new employee at the wage stated on the labor certification application. The priority date for quota-waiting begins when the labor certification application is filed with the state job service.

Keeping Your Green Card

After going through the time, effort, expense and heartache of obtaining a green card, did you know that a green card can be lost without its holder doing anything wrong? This does not include the rare instances when one forfeits a green card by committing a felony or serious crime.

Once in possession of a green card you must make the U.S. your permanent residence, meaning that you must live in the U.S. The INS often questions green card holders at ports of entry and asks when they last visited the U.S. If you work abroad and make only one or two short trips to the U.S. each year, the INS will assume that you live abroad unless proven otherwise. If you cannot prove that you live in the U.S., the INS inspector will confiscate your green card at the port of entry and you'll have to go to court to get it back.

Green card holders must prove they live in the U.S.,

while nonimmigrant visa holders must prove they don't live in the U.S. Living in the U.S. means making the U.S. your primary and permanent residence. The INS considers factors such as having a residence, bank account, driver's license, credit cards, regular bills and registered vehicle, and filing U.S. income tax returns. You do not have to own a residence; you may rent or live with a relative. The INS looks at all the facts and makes a judgment call as there is no clear definition of living in the U.S. Instead, it is a matter of facts and circumstances.

Re-entry Permits

If you need to leave the U.S. for more than six months, we recommend applying for a Permit to Re-enter. The application for this permit affords you the opportunity to explain the reason for a temporary absence from the U.S., and to make a formal declaration that you do not intend to relinquish your permanent U.S. residence. You must also agree to file U.S. income tax returns. INS approval gives you permission to remain abroad for up to two years without risking loss of the green card.

File the Permit to Re-enter (Form I-131) at an appropriate INS regional processing center. Expect a 120-day processing period. You must be in the U.S. during the processing period. The INS will not give you permission to return to the U.S. if you've already left. For those already abroad, there is a similar embassy procedure.

It's acceptable to explain that you were transferred abroad by your employer or that you have business abroad, and upon the conclusion of your assignment you intend to return to the U.S.

The re-entry permit itself is a travel document. It contains your picture along with spaces for visas and entry and exit stamps. Re-entry permits are valid for two years and may be renewed. Persons holding Taiwanese or other passports that aren't likely to be recognized often use the re-entry permit as a travel document, instead of a passport.

If you live abroad, hold a permit to re-enter and do not file income tax returns, the INS may confiscate your green card at a port of entry. Permission to live abroad without relinquishing a permanent U.S. residence is conditioned upon filing U.S. income tax returns.

Remember, once you have the green card, no matter where you live, keep it until the INS takes it away. There is no requirement to return the green card to the INS. The INS must prove its case before your permanent residence status is lost.

Tax Returns

U.S. tax laws require green card holders and American citizens to file tax returns and report income earned anywhere in the world. Tax treaties and credits for taxes paid to foreign governments usually eliminate double taxation. Immigrants from low-tax jurisdictions should consider the tax costs of maintaining a permanent U.S. residence. The tax dollars, in part, pay for the services that make the U.S. a desirable place to live. There is a price for everything!

The Internal Revenue Service (IRS) and INS exchange information. For example, the INS reports all new green card approvals to the IRS, and both agencies maintain staff in foreign countries. The IRS will try to locate tax cheats; tax problems usually result in immigration problems. Although the lack of administrative resources prevents full-scale searches, random checks and tips from disgruntled citizens, personal enemies and jilted spouses often provide the INS and IRS with useful information.

Failure to file a tax return violates U.S. tax laws but not immigration statutes. There is no immigration law that requires aliens to pay American taxes. However, the INS considers filing a tax return as important evidence of one's intention to maintain a permanent U.S. residence. The tax issue may arise in two ways:

Permits to Re-enter

The Permit to Re-enter form requires the applicant to promise to file U.S. income tax returns. Failure to file may result in denial of subsequent re-entry permit applications or loss of the re-entry permit, not necessarily loss of the green card.

INS inspectors at ports of entry occasionally ask re-entry permit holders if they have filed U.S. tax returns. If the answer is no, they may confiscate the re-entry permit. The INS inspector may also question whether the applicant has maintained a permanent U.S. residence.

INS processing centers routinely ask re-entry permit applicants if they filed U.S. tax returns. If the answer is negative, the INS will deny the permit application. In this case, there is little risk of losing the green card as the applicant must be present in the U.S. to apply for the re-entry permit. It's difficult for the INS to revoke a green card petition when the applicant is already in the U.S.

Green Card

A U.S. permanent resident who lives full-time in America but does not file U.S. income tax returns will not lose his green card, as the U.S. is clearly his permanent residence. This person, however, may have problems with the IRS, not the INS.

On the other hand, a U.S. permanent resident who lives abroad for six months or more and fails to file tax returns may have problems with both the IRS and INS. In addition to the time spent overseas, failure to file tax returns indicates that the U.S. isn't the place of permanent residence.

When Tax & Immigration Laws Conflict

Many green card holders using tax treaty elections choose to file tax returns abroad instead of in the U.S. Since tax treaties supercede U.S. domestic law, one may technically make a tax treaty election without causing a problem with the IRS or INS. Yet immigration laws view U.S. tax returns as important evidence of permanent residence status.

What happens when the tax and immigration laws conflict? Simply put, the American judicial system has not definitively answered this question. However, common sense suggests that if the immigration benefit is more important than avoiding U.S. tax payments, pay the tax and don't create a fight with the INS. One can argue with the INS as a citizen without risking citizenship. But you can't argue with the INS as a permanent resident without risking loss of green card. Put another way, the IRS only wants to collect taxes—a matter of money, while the INS controls whether the individual will reside in the U.S.A.—a matter of residence. Anyone who wants to be a permanent American resident should file U.S. income tax returns.

An Example of Green Card Forfeiture

The most common way to lose a green card is to move

back to an overseas home and make only short trips to the U.S. This happens most often to executives, managers and businesspeople. For example, "Mr. Smith" transfers to an overseas office while leaving his wife and children to finish school in the U.S. The husband commutes to visit his family. So far so good.

Mrs. Smith moves to join her husband overseas, while one child stays in the U.S. to continue schooling. The Smiths pay American income taxes but do not maintain a residence. They stay with one of their children while in the U.S, and their car and bills are in the child's name. Smith and his wife intend to resume living in the U.S. once Smith retires.

During one of the Smiths' visits to their children, the INS questions them at the airport and learns the truth. The INS asks Mr. Smith if he has a Re-entry Permit? Since Smith doesn't have a re-entry permit he'll probably lose his green card. If Smith had a re-entry permit, he wouldn't have experienced problems. He also should have taken a few other precautions. If he had planned correctly, the house, car and bills would have remained in his name. In other words, the children should have been living in Mr. Smith's house, not the other way around.

The revocation of Mr. Smith's green card does not mean that his children lose their green cards. Although children may obtain green cards through parents, they do not lose green cards simply because the parents lost their's. Adult children can petition for the parents at any time, and if the child is a citizen, there is no quota wait. If Mr. Smith has no other qualifying relatives in the U.S., he may take the matter to court or hope his company transfers him to the U.S. again.

Summary

- Green card holders must make the U.S. their primary and permanent residence.

- Tax laws, not immigration laws, require filing U.S. tax returns.

- Filing tax returns is evidence of U.S. permanent residence for immigration law purposes.

- Re-entry permit allows extended absences abroad.

- Re-entry permit holders must file U.S. tax returns as a condition for permission to remain abroad for extended periods.

Chapter 9

Student Visas

Students use F-1 visas for academic programs and M-1 visas for vocational programs. To be eligible for either of these visas the student must first be accepted by a school.

Once the student is accepted, the school will prepare Form I-20 for the student to submit to the INS or to a consulate. The I-20 Form provides information about the student's course of study and his means of financial support.

General Procedures

Students use F-1 visas for academic programs and M-1 visas for vocational programs. The key difference between the two categories is that M-1 holders may not change to another nonimmigrant status while in the U.S. Generally, both visa categories are issued for the duration of the approved educational program. In both cases, visa procedures may be initiated from the U.S. or abroad. The procedure for obtaining an F-1 student visa is as follows:

Step 1. Be accepted by a school.

Step 2. Obtain Form I-20 from the school. Form I-20 details the proposed course of study and estimates the financial resources necessary to complete the course of study.

Step 3. If in the U.S., send Form I-506 Change of Status, Form I-20, and proof of financial support to the appropriate INS Regional Processing Center. If the INS approves the petition, the INS will respond with an endorsed I-94 evidencing student status. If abroad, fill out the consular application forms, supply Form I-20 from the school as well as proof of financial support. The consul will signify approval by issuing an F-1 or M-1 visa.

Travel on a Student Visa

All students who wish to leave the U.S. must obtain an endorsed Form I-20ID from a designated school official each time they leave the U.S. The school's endorsement proves that the student is still in school and making satisfactory progress under the approved educational program.

Students who try to enter the U.S. with a student visa but without an endorsed I-20ID risk denial of entry. At a minimum, they must convince the INS at the port of entry of their intentions to maintain an approved course of study.

Students may travel without a visa—provided they have a valid I-94 and an endorsed I-20ID—to Canada or Mexico for up to 30 days. All other overseas destinations require a visa. This means that the student who obtained student status in the U.S. must ultimately return home to obtain a visa if they want to leave North America and re-enter.

Financial Support

Students must prove a source of adequate financial support. Parents, guardians or benefactors should supply an Affidavit of Support, Form I-134, and supply proof of sufficient funds to support the student for the duration of the approved course of study. The person signing the Affidavit of Support guarantees the student will not use public assistance or welfare. Theoretically, this is rarely enforced; the signer of the I-134 is responsible for reimbursing the government in the event the student uses public assistance.

Strict Enforcement

Since many students drop out of school, work illegally or never attend classes, the INS and consuls carefully monitor F-1 or M-1 applications. Good students attending academically-respected institutions experience few difficulties. But students with average or poor grades, along with English as second-language school applicants, experience greater scrutiny. The consuls and INS want to make sure the student indends to study and not use the student visa to disappear in the U.S. Students must prove their credibility.

Where to Get Assistance

American schools often charge foreign students higher tuitions. Indeed, some schools depend on foreign student tuition for their financial survival. Somewhere near every major American university are residences, dormitories or companies devoted to assisting the various nationalities of the college's foreign students.

Although one may always consult with an attorney, several private companies provide care and support for foreign students and will assist with visa processing. Such companies routinely care for overseas students and often help convince the consul of a student's good standing, as well as his or her intention to study while in the U.S.

Three Key Questions Need The Same Answer: Yes

The consuls and INS ask three key questions when reviewing student visa applications. These questions, along with the recommended answers, are listed below.

1. Do you intend to complete a full-time course of study?

Be prepared to submit past school records and letters of recommendation from teachers as evidence.

2. Do you have financial support?

Produce proof of adequate funds and/or show the financial statement of a sponsor on Form I-134, Affavidit of

Support.

3. Will you return to your home country after your studies are completed?

Prove this intention by demonstrating close family ties in your home country and/or a network of friends, relatives or job prospects. A course of study related to a prospective job in your home country also helps indicate your plans to return. For example, the father owns a ski lodge and resort and sends his child to the U.S. to study hotel management. In this case, the job logically relates to the course of study.

Working While Studying

The following programs allow students to work while attending a school in the U.S.

On-Campus Employment

Any full-time student in good academic standing may work 20 hours a week at an on-campus facility during the school year, and full-time between quarters or semesters.

Pilot Off-Campus Employment Program

This program permits 20 hours a week of off-campus employment at a private business. Onerous paperwork and recruitment requirements often deter employers from this program.

Curricular Practical Training

This training must be offered in connection with a field of study. Generally, students must arrange curricular practical training with academic advisors and the school processing the necessary paperwork. Students who work for a year or longer in this program lose eligibility for post-completion practical training.

Post-Completion Practical Training Program

This popular program permits students to work off-campus for one year after completion of all degree requirements. Application for this program must be made between 90 days before and 30 days after completion of a course of study. To become eligible for this program, first find a job and then seek the school's approval of the employment. The school files the necessary forms with the INS.

After INS approval, obtain an Employment Authorization Card (Form I-765) to work legally. File Form I-765 and go to the nearest INS office for photographing. The Employment Authorization Card should be available in one or two days.

Students cannot leave the U.S. after graduation and then apply for post-completion practical training. Practical training must be approved *before* leaving the U.S., and students may travel after practical training approval. Students have 60 days from the end of the practical training period to depart the U.S., resume studies or change to another visa status.

Options After Practical Training

Students hoping to stay in the U.S. after practical training have few options. They can get married to a U.S. citizen,π or find a job and apply for an H-1B or an E visa. Recent university graduates usually qualify as professionals for H-1B status. Experience is not a requirement for H-1B visa professional or specialty-worker status.

Students may qualify for E visa status if they are hired by a treaty company controlled by members of their nationality. For example, a Japanese student could obtain an E visa as a professional or manager through a Japanese-owned company.

Quite often, students and employers assume that E visas only apply to transferees from the treaty country, as when managers transfer from the home office to a U.S. subsidiary. A treaty company may hire any qualified treaty national even if they were not previously employed by a related company abroad.

Chapter 10

Visas for the Privileged, Media, Athletes, Entertainers, Cultural Exchanges, Religious Workers & Tycoons

Several lesser-used nonimmigrant visa categories deserve discussion.

These include I visas for persons working in information media; O visas for outstanding artists, businesspeople, chefs and their support staff; P visas for professional athletes, musical groups and entertainers; Q visas for cultural exchanges; and R visas for religious workers.

I Visa for Information Media

The I visa permits employees of foreign information media engaged in news-gathering or documentary material, along with key staff such as film crews and editors, to work in the U.S. Independent production companies qualify as long as the journalists hold credentials issued by a journalistic association. The I visa does not require university degrees or existing U.S. trade or business. The focus is on information-gathering and reporting for news or documentary purposes, not entertainment.

An example of who's eligible for the I visa might include a foreign television station that wishes to send a journalist and editor to the U.S. to collect material for documentary segments on American lifestyles. The journalist had over 10 years experience and a press card, but no university degree. The foreign television station agreed to support the journalist while in the U.S. This case was approved.

We have processed I visas for a radio show covering U.S. lifestyle, a travelogue, a documentary discussion of Marilyn Monroe photos, as well as a Super Bowl play-by-play announcer. In all cases the applicants reported newsworthy events or created educational or documentary shows.

O Visa for Oustanding Actors, Businesspeople & Artists

The O category helps people with extraordinary skills obtain visas. We often use the category as an alternative to

H-1B for persons with no university degree. The O visa most commonly permits key actors and technical staff to work for motion picture, television and stage productions. Individual athletes, scientists, educators and tycoons may also qualify for O visas. We've used O visas for actors, artists, computer graphics designers in the television industry, and others. I'm proud to report that one of my O visa clients designed some of the commercials used during the 1994 Super Bowl telecast.

We've used O-1 visas to permit the producer, key technical staff and actors to come to Seattle, Washington, for the filming of the movie, "The Little Buddha." The producer, director, art people, cameramen and other key technicians had international experience and easily qualified for O-1 visa status. We filed O-2 petitions for the supporting actors and assistants.

O visa applicants must obtain letters from an industry's professional organization and a labor organization attesting to their outstanding qualifications. It must be stated that there is no objection to granting a visa to the aliens. Unions often resist providing favorable letters if they believe qualified American workers exist. The maximum validity period is three years.

The O visa category can be used by just about anyone who's famous or internationally acclaimed in a recognized field of endeavor. Consider this category when the visa candidate does not have a university degree. Remember, the applicant must either be famous or possess esoteric skills. Otherwise, labor unions won't issue favorable advisory opinions.

P Visa for Sports Teams, Athletes & Entertainment Groups

The P visa works, as a practical matter, the same as the O visa except that it applies to athletes and entertainment groups. For example, a Bunraku or Japanese puppet troupe would use P visas for the puppeteers, readers and key support staff. P visas also apply to athletic teams, boxers, sumo wrestlers and ethnic dance troupes. Validity periods depend on the length of the engagements, not to exceed five years.

Q Visa for Cultural Exchange Programs

Q visas are for cultural exchange programs which provide a sharing of history, culture or traditions of the alien's country of nationality. The Q visa cultural exchange program must be designed to exhibit the history, culture, religion, attitudes, philosophy or traditions of the alien's home country. The alien's employment must be connected to making the cultural exchange program work. One of our Q visa cases was a program hosted by an Indian restaurant that exhibited the traditions, philosophy and preparation of regional Indian cooking. The Indian restaurant used a Q visa to hire a chef to run the program. Validity periods depend on the length of the engagements, generally not to exceed 15 months.

R Visa Religious Workers

At least some members of virtually every ethnic group in the world live in the U.S. Consider that members of any particular ethnic group divide their loyalties among several different religions. Some religions have nothing to do with ethnic affiliation, while others cater to a particular ethnic group.

For example, in Seattle, Washington, there is a Finnish Lutheran Church, a Swedish Lutheran Church and many other nonethnic Lutheran churches. While all Lutherans, there is a special church council or governing body for the Finns and another for the Swedes. The Finns and Swedes prefer ministers who speak the native language and are trained in native customs. Many other churches, temples and synagogues have the same preference. The R visa for religious occupations satisfies this purpose.

Religious institutions catering to a particular ethnic group often make that group's members more comfortable by providing a minister or religious workers from the home country to perform services and other religious and cultural activities.

Ministers

There are no particular education requirements for an R visa. The applicant must have been a member of the church or religious organization for at least two years prior to application. The application procedure is very simple. Apply through the INS application, or application can be made directly to the consul by letter. The visa is usually valid for three years with a two-year extension. The R visa is very flexible and available to all religions. There is also a green card category available to religious workers. The requirements are very similar to the R visa, and religious workers are exempt from labor certification.

I never gave this category much thought until a few years ago when we helped Buddhist nuns from Taiwan. I assumed that any woman who shaved her head, wore a nondescript saffron robe, and bore ritual tattoos and burn marks could be considered a legitimate Buddhist. I was wrong. The INS gently informed me that Taiwanese and Thai businessmen and women, in particular, often give large donations to a temple, disguise themselves as monks or nuns, and apply for an R visa and then a green card as a religious worker. Very clever. This is an abused category, so be prepared to carefully document your religious convictions and affiliation. The more strict consuls require ritual by fire.

When a pastor of the Finnish Lutheran Church in Seattle passed away, the church members wanted a Finnish replacement. The new replacement was ordained by the governing body of the church, studied religion at the university level, and had over two years experience. The church is a nonprofit religious organization. This case more than met the legal requirements for an R visa. Although ministers do not have to graduate from a university, they must be ordained or be able to prove they have authority to conduct religious worship. Religious workers also need two years experience with a particular religious organization immediately prior to transfer to the U.S.

Religious Workers

Another case arose when a religious outreach program, again Lutheran, needed a social worker to direct an outreach program to help refugees from Somalia, Eritrea and Ethiopia. The refugees were having trouble adjusting to life in the U.S., and the church-sponsored outreach program provided social and religious counseling services as well as religious training. The program did not require a minister but needed a social worker with Lutheran training.

The applicant had a Nursing degree plus two years of religious training and over two years experience providing religious comfort to sick people in Lutheran hospitals in

Finland. The applicant had worked for a Lutheran hospital for over two years. This applicant's credentials exceeded the minimum requirements.

R visa religious workers may include counselors, social workers, health-care workers for religious hospitals, missionaries, translators, religious broadcasters and just about any other occupation necessary to a religious organization. The term "religious worker" does not include janitors, fundraisers and people removed from the religion. An exception to this is seen in the few religions where the janitor must follow religious practices.

Details About NAFTA

The North American Free Trade Agreement (NAFTA) provides additional nonimmigrant visa categories—mostly for professional workers (designated TN)—for citizens of Mexico and Canada to work in the U.S. The reverse applies for U.S. citizens wishing to work in Mexico or Canada. The complete list of NAFTA categories is available from the U.S., Canadian or Mexico consulates. The list is also available in the Federal Register, Site 8C.F.R., Section 214.6(c).

Additionally under NAFTA, Canadians may apply for L-1 or H-1 status at specified land border crossings or airports. Mexicans must continue to apply through INS regional processing centers. For Canadians, the NAFTA filing procedures avoid processing delays incurred at INS regional processing centers.

Expedited Procedures for Canadians under NAFTA

Canadian TN applicants may apply at land border ports of entry and designated airports. Applications simply consist of a cover letter explaining eligibility for the particular category and documented proof, such as university transcripts or verification of required experience. No additional forms are necessary. Border processing usually occurs on the spot, and generally takes no longer than a couple of days. The INS evidences Treaty National status by issuing an I-94 card endorsed "TN."

All Treaty Nationals may work in the U.S. for periods of up to one year, and TN status may be renewed annually. Although NAFTA does not limit the number of extensions available to TN visa holders, common sense dictates that the INS will question frequent extension applicants.

Strategy

The NAFTA visas afford Canadians fast processing— with minimal paperwork—when the system works. Processing procedures and policies vary among the border-crossing posts. Some posts process petitions on the spot while others prefer to review copies before interviewing the applicant. Enforcement policies also vary; some posts are stricter than others. Since the situation constantly changes, we advise NAFTA applicants to check for local procedures before applying at a border post.

Most NAFTA applicants also qualify for H, L or E visa status. NAFTA works for those who wish to work in the U.S. for a short period of time, or for those who need to quickly start work in America. Once in the U.S., NAFTA applicants may change to a longer-term nonimmigrant visa, such as H-1, E-1/2 or L-1A.

Chapter 11

Naturalization: Becoming An American Citizen

Most countries of the world base citizenship on parentage, and try to limit citizenship to particular ethnic heritage.

For example, a person born in Japan or France must have a Japanese or French parent to become a citizen. Many countries require a male qualifying parent, while a few nations require a female qualifying parent. Recently, many countries have eliminated the sex discrimination but retained the parentage requirement.

America, a country open to all ethnic groups, automatically grants citizenship to any person born in the U.S., regardless of parental nationality and why or how long the parents were in the country. Persons born in America merely need to present a birth certificate to apply for a passport. Otherwise, U.S. citizenship, with few exceptions, requires the passage of time as a green card resident, basic knowledge of U.S. history and government, and an ability to speak English.

Because many people plan to give birth to a child in the U.S. (for automatic citizenship), there is some talk about requiring a greater than nine-month residency requirement. (This is known in the trade as "baby droppers.")

People over 55 who've resided in the U.S. for 20 years or more do not have to meet the language requirement. After all, how does someone live in the U.S. for 20 years and avoid learning English? Amazingly, such people do exist.

Advantages of Citizenship

There are two practical advantages of U.S. citizenship: You can vote, and it's hard to lose citizen status. You can lose citizenship if you lied to get a green card, failed to disclose past crimes, or perjured a material fact relating to citizenship or a green card. Unlike aliens who can lose their green card as a result of prolonged absence from the U.S.,

American citizens may leave the country and return at any time without fear of losing citizenship.

Every American citizen can vote. Since permanent residents are taxpayers, they want to have a say about the amount of income tax and how it's spent. There are many other important reasons to vote.

Dual Citizenship

The U.S. permits dual nationality. American citizens of dual nationality must consult the other country about holding two passports. The U.S. government does not inquire or even care if a person owns two passports. For example, a U.S. citizen holding U.S. and Japanese passports may risk losing his Japanese passport to the Japanese government, but not the U.S. passport.

The Qualifying Period

A green card spouse of a U.S. citizen must reside in the U.S. for three years before becoming eligible for citizenship. All other permanent residents must reside in the U.S. for five years. If your American spouse dies while you have a green card, you still may qualify under the three-year rule.

One must live in the U.S. six months or more in each consecutive year. With few exceptions, a break in residence restarts the qualifying period at the beginning. If you work abroad without obtaining a re-entry permit and return seven months later, you will lose the year for citizenship-qualifying purposes, and must begin the qualification period over.

A hypothetical example of this is seen when a green card graduate student goes abroad for a year of field work without obtaining a re-entry permit. While abroad, the student remains registered with an American university. The one year abroad breaks the citizenship qualification period, and the student must wait five more years before applying for citizenship. Obtaining a re-entry permit would have prevented restarting the qualifying period, but time abroad would not have counted.

The Citizenship Test

Upon meeting the residency requirements, one may file for naturalization at any INS District Office. File the appropriate form (N-400), which includes biographical information and proof of required residence. The INS will schedule an interview for the person to be tested on U.S. history and government. Only those who meet the 55-20 requirement (be 55 years or older and have 20 years of residency in the U.S.) will avoid being tested in English. English language ability is a citizenship requirement.

The test questions are the same sorts of things most Americans learn in junior high schools. Several books are available in libraries and book stores to provide sample questions and study aids. Most immigration examiners ask reasonable questions. Examiners tend to ask difficult questions when they suspect the applicant did not study. Sample questions could include:

"Do you know how many congressmen comprise the Senate and House of Representatives?"

"Can you name the first five Presidents in order?"

"Do you know who was the president of the Confederacy?"

INS examiners tend to be understanding of those who studied for the test. When asked "Who was George Washington?," one of my clients answered, "My first son." Confused, the elderly woman, with help from the INS examiner, managed to regain her composure and pass the test. In another case, a young Chinese woman, laden with gold jewelry and who obviously didn't study, was rejected after she failed to identify the metal responsible for the California Gold Rush. (By the way, the Chinese characters for San Francisco translate to "Gold Mountain.") This woman had made no attempt to learn English, and the examiner was looking for a way for her to fail the test.

Certificate of Naturalization

Upon passing the citizenship test and residency requirements, a citizenship paper (called the "Certificate of Naturalization") can be obtained from the INS or a federal court. Name changes are permissable at the time of naturalization, if so desired.

The INS procedure is faster, and the federal court procedure, scheduled every few months, is more elaborate. In the court procedure, the judge says a few kind words, the citizenship candidates pledge allegiance to the U.S., and they then receive naturalization certificates.

Many people prefer the more elaborate federal court ceremony to commemorate this important personal event. On the 4th of July, Independence Day in the U.S., most American cities hold a large citizenship ceremony. People from all over the world, with different backgrounds, experiences and personal stories of how they came to the U.S., become American citizens at the same time. We call this American phenomena the "melting pot," whereby people from all over the world become citizens of the United States of America.

Appendices

A. Glossary

B. Immigration Forms & Other Documents

C. Visa Categories

D. Important Addresses

E. Suggested Document Lists

F. Proposed Changes In U.S. Immigration Law

A. Glossary

Please refer to the Glossary for answers to any questions about the specialized terms used in this book.

Adjustment of Status: The procedures for changing to permanent residence status through the INS.

Advance Parole: Permission to leave the U.S. and re-enter during adjustment of status procedures.

Application for Immigrant Visa and Alien Registration: The procedures for applying for immigrant status through a consulate.

Bilateral Investment Treaty, Friendship Commerce and Navigation Treaties: The agreements between the U.S. and a foreign government which enable treaty trader or treaty investor status.

Change of Status: An application to the INS to change from one nonimmigrant status to another nonimmigrant status.

Consulates: Representative offices of a foreign country located in major cities of the host country. Consulates take care of trade, economic, political and visa issues.

Consuls: Foreign service employees who work in Embassies and Consulates. Consuls issue visas.

Department of State: The agency of the United States government responsible for managing its foreign affairs. This agency controls the issuance of visas for travel to the U.S.

Embassy: The representative office of a foreign country located in the capital city of the host country. Embassies take care of political, trade, economic and visa issues. An Ambassador is the head of post at an Embassy.

Essential Skill: A skill, essential to the success of the enterprise, that is generally unavailable in the U.S.

Executive: The person who establishes corporate goals and policies, and monitors the managers.

Extension of Stay: An application to the INS to extend the stay period listed on Form I-94.

I-94 Card: The form issued to temporary visitors to the U.S. that evidences their immigration status and allowed period of stay within the U.S.

Immigrant: A person who wants to live in the U.S. for an indefinite period of time or permanently.

Immigration and Naturalization Service (INS): A sub-agency of the U.S. Department of Justice responsible for controlling immigration within the U.S.

International Organization: A foreign and U.S. company(s) linked by 50 percent or more common ownership.

Labor Certification: The process for determining that no U.S. workers meet the offered job's minimum requirements. Unless exempted, labor certification is a prerequisite for employment-based green card categories.

Labor Conditions Application Process: A form filed with the Department of Labor for the purpose of notifying U.S. workers that a foreign worker will be employed at the job site. Also used for the purpose of ensuring that the U.S. employer is not hiring a foreign worker at less than the wages normally paid to U.S. workers for the same position.

Manager: A person who manages other managers, supervisors or professionals within a business organization. Managers implement corporate goals and policies through subordinates.

Naturalization: The process for becoming a U.S. citizen.

Nonimmigrant Status: A temporary status limited to a particular purpose for a set period of time.

Petition: Generic name for the forms used by the INS to determine eligibility for various visa categories.

Prevailing Wage: The wage, determined by the Department of Labor, normally paid to U.S. workers for a particular job.

Practical Training: A program available to students that permits them to work in the U.S. after or during university study.

Quota System: The system used to limit the number of visas available to each country for particular visa classifications.

Pilot Visa Waiver Program: An agreement with several countries and the U.S. that permits each other's nationals to enter the country for business or pleasure purposes without a visa for up to 90 days.

Professionals: Persons with at least a four-year university degree, or equivalent in experience and education, in a recognized professional discipline, such as accounting, law, engineering or the sciences.

Re-entry Permit: A declaration of one's intention to maintain U.S. permanent residence during prolonged absences from the U.S.

Specialized Knowledge: A narrowly-held skill which helps the U.S. employer's ability to compete in international markets.

Treaty Investment: Substantial investment in the U.S. made by treaty companies or individuals.

Treaty Trade: Substantial trade between the U.S. and a foreign country.

Visa: Permission to apply for entry to a country, usually issued by a country's foreign service.

Visa Revalidation: An application to the Visa Office in Washington D.C. for a new visa of the same type.

142

B. Immigration Forms & Other Documents

Forms Requiring No Filing Fees

The following forms require no filing fees. Forms are available from the U.S. Government Printing Office or a local INS office.

Form Number	Title
ETA 750, part A & B	Application for Labor Certification
ETA-9035	Labor Condition Application (part of H-1B filing)
G-325	Biographical (usually used in the U.S. only)
I-9	Confirmation of Authority to Work
OF-156	Visa Application/Revalidation
OF-179	Document Checklist (Embassy)
OF-230, part 1 & 2	Biographical (Embassy)

Forms Requiring Fees

Since filing fees change frequently, we won't include them in this book. For an updated Fee List, contact an INS center.

Form Number	Title
I-17	Petition for Approval of School for Attendance by Nonimmigrant Students
I-90	Application to Replace Alien Registration Card

Form Number	Title
I-102	Application for Replacement/ Initial Nonimmigrant Arrival-Departure Document
I-129	Petition for Nonimmigrant Worker
I-129E	Supplement
I-129F	Petition for Alien Fiance(e)
I-129H	Supplement
I-129L	Supplement
I-130	Petition for Alien Relative
I-131	Application for Travel Document/ Request for Advance Parole
I-140	Petition for Prospective Immigrant Employee
I-191	Application for Advance Permission to Return to Unrelinquished Domicile
I-192	Application for Advanced Permission to Enter as Nonimmigrant
I-193	Application for Waiver of Passport and/or Visa
I-212	Application for Permission to Reapply for Admission into the United States After Deportation or Removal
I-246	Application for Stay of Deportation

Form Number	Title
I-256A	Application for Suspension of Deportation
I-290	A Notice of Appeal to the Board of Immigration Appeals
I-290B	Notice of Appeal to the Administrative Appeal Unit
I-360	Petition for Amerasian, Widow(er), or Special Immigrant (except there is no fee for a petition seeking classification as an Amerasian)
I-485	Application for Permanent Resident
I-526	Immigrant Petition by Alien Entrepreneur
I-539	Application to Extend/Change Nonimmigrant Status
I-600	Petition to Classify Orphan as an Immediate Relative
I-600A	Application for Advance Processing of Orphan Petition
I-601	Application for Waiver of Grounds of Excludability
I-612	Application for Waiver of the Foreign Residence Requirement
I-690	Application for Waiver of Grounds of Excludability

Form Number	Title
I-694	Notice of Appeal of Decision under Section 210 or 245A of the Immigration and Nationality Act
I-695	Application for Replacement of Form I-688A, Employment Authorization for Form I-688, Temporary Residence Card
I-698	Application to Adjust Status from Temporary to Permanent Resident
I-751	Petition to Remove the Conditions of Residence
I-765	Application for Employment Authorization
I-817	Application for Voluntary Departure Under the Family Unity Program
I-821	Application for Temporary Protected Status
I-823	Application for Participation in a Dedicated Commuter Lane Program
I-824	Application for Action on an Approved Application or Petition
Motions	Motions to Reopen or Reconsider
N-300	Application to File Declaration of Intention
N-336	Request for Hearing on a Decision Naturalization Processing

Form Number	Title
N-400	Application for Naturalization
N-410	Motion for Amendment of Petition (Application)
N-455	Application for Transfer of Petition for Naturalization
N-470	Application to Preserve Residence for Naturalization Purposes
N-565	Application for Replacement Naturalization Purposes
N-600	Application for Certificate of Citizenship
N-643	Application for Certificate of Citizenship in Behalf of an Adopted Child
N-644	Application for Posthumous Citizenship

C. Visa Categories

Nonimmigrant Visa Categories

Here is a list of all the nonimmigrant visa categories. Some of the lesser-used categories have been combined into one description. All visa categories are designated by letters of the alphabet. Subcategories are designated by numbers. For example, L is the letter designating visas for international organizations. L-1 is for the principal applicant, L-2 is for dependents. "Dependents" means spouse and children under 21 years of age.

A-1 through A-3. Diplomats, public ministers, dependents and personal attendants.

B-1. Business visitors.

B-2. Tourist visitors.

C-1. Travelers in transit through the U.S.

D-1. Airline or ship crew.

E-1. Treaty trader.

E-2. Treaty investor.

F-1. Academic and language training students.

G-1 through G-5. Representatives of foreign governments and employees of quasi-governmental international organizations and some United Nations employees, servants and dependents.

NATO-1 through NATO-5. Certain employees and military personnel of the North Atlantic Treaty Organization, dependents and servants.

H-1A. Registered nurses.

H-1B. Specialty occupations and professionals.

H-2A. Temporary or seasonal agricultural workers unavailable in the U.S.

H-2B. Other temporary or seasonal workers unavailable in the U.S.

H-3. Temporary trainees learning skills unavailable in their home country.

H-4. Immediate family of H visa classifications.

I. Foreign press and information media coming to report on newsworthy or informational events as opposed to selling entertainment.

J-1. Exchange visitors coming as part of a United States Information Agency-approved exchange program.

J-2. Dependents of J visa holders.

K-1. Fiancees of U.S. citizens who intend to marry within 90 days of entry.

L-1. Intracompany transferees in an executive, managerial or specialized knowledge capacity.

L-2. L-1 dependents.

M-1. Vocational school students.

M-2. M-1 dependents.

O-1. Individuals of extraordinary ability in the arts, sciences, business, professions or athletics.

O-2. Essential support staff of O-1 aliens.

O-3. O visa dependents.

P-1. Internationally-renowned artists, athletes and entertainers and their support staff.

P-2. Entertainers coming to perform at a government-approved cultural exchange program.

P-3. Culturally-unique entertainers.

P-4.   P visa dependents.

Q-1.   Participants in international cultural exchange pro-
       grams; may be privately-sponsored.

Q-2.   Q visa dependents.

R-1.   Ministers and religious workers.

R-2.   R visa dependents.

S.   International terrorist informants.

TN.   North American Free Trade Agreement (NAFTA)
       nationals.

Permanent Resident Visa Categories

Family-Sponsored Preferences

First Preference: Unmarried sons and daughters of citizens.

Second Preference: Spouses and children, and unmarried sons
and daughters of permanent residents.

Third Preference: Married sons and daughters of citizens.

Fourth Preference: Brothers and sisters of adult citizens.

Employment-Based Preferences

First Preference: Priority workers, international managers.

Second Preference: Members of professions holding advanced
degrees or persons of exceptional ability.

Third Preference: Skilled workers, professionals and other
workers.

Fourth Preference: Certain special immigrants.

Fifth Preference: Employment creation.

D. Important Addresses

Immigration & Naturalization Service Centers

Eastern

The Eastern INS Service Center has jurisdiction over the following states: Massachusetts, Connecticut, New Hampshire, Rhode Island, New York, Pennsylvania, Delaware, Washington D.C., West Virginia, Maryland, New Jersey, Virginia, Maine and Vermont.

It also has jurisdiction over the following INS offices: Puerto Rico, Bermuda, Toronto, Montreal, Virgin Islands and Dominican Republic.

Eastern INS Service Center

75 Lower Welden Street

St. Albans, VT 05479-0001

Phone: (802) 527-3160

Northern

The Northern INS Service Center has jurisdiction over the following states: Michigan, Illinois, Indiana, Wisconsin, Oregon, Alaska, Minnesota, North Dakota, South Dakota, Kansas, Missouri, Washington, Idaho, Colorado, Utah, Wyoming, Ohio, Nebraska and Iowa.

It also has jurisdiction over the following INS offices: Manitoba, British Columbia and Calgary.

Northern INS Service Center

Federal Building and U.S. Courthouse

850 "S" Street

Lincoln, NE 68501

Phone: (402) 437-5218 or (402) 437-5464

Southern

The Southern INS Service Center has jurisdiction over the following states: Florida, Texas, New Mexico, Oklahoma, Georgia, North Carolina, South Carolina, Alabama, Louisiana, Arkansas, Mississippi, Tennessee and Kentucky.

It also has jurisdiction over the following INS offices: Bahamas, Freeport and Nassau.

Southern INS Service Center

PO Box 15122

Department "A"

Irving, TX 75015-2122

Phone: (214) 767-7769

Western

The Western INS Service Center has jurisdiction over the following states and territory: California, Hawaii, Arizona, Nevada and Guam.

For expedite and courier deliveries:

Western INS Service Center

24000 Avila Road

2nd Floor, Room 2304

Laguna Niguel, CA 92677

Attn: Incoming Mailroom

For regular mail:

PO Box 30111

Laguna Niguel, CA 92677-8011

Consulates

Each foreign country has its own consular office. Look in your local telephone directory for the consulate nearest you.

Visa Office

U.S. Visa Office
2401 East Street N.W.
Washington, D.C. 20520

E. Suggested Document Lists

Here are the suggested document lists for the various visa applications. The documents listed are necessary for background information for a particular visa petition.

E-1 Treaty Trader Visa Application

1. *Information concerning parent company:*

   a. Articles of Incorporation, seal page only

   b. Financial Statement

   c. Company brochure and general description of business

   d. Organizational chart, number of employees and general job titles

   e. Business goal in the U.S.

   f. Shareholders, percent ownership and nationality

   g. In case of holding companies, supply description of business activities of principal investors or shareholder.

2. *Information concerning the U.S. company or enterprise:*

   a. Articles of Incorporation and organizational documents

   b. Financial Statement and Pro Forma for start-up

   c. Description of business goals in the U.S.

   d. U.S. organizational chart and staffing requirements

   e. Evidence of initial and continuing investment; i.e., currency transfers and invoices

   f. Job description of transferee

g. Amount and proof of trade between the U.S. and foreign company; i.e., invoices, shipping document samples, in-house accounting, computer, etc.

h. Proof of U.S. investment, trade activities, invoices, currency transfers, etc.

3. **Information concerning the Alien:**

a. Personal data, name, date of birth, address in foreign country in last two years

b. Resumé detailing complete employment history with salaries for recent jobs

c. Educational history

d. Biographical details regarding accompanying family members, if any.

E-2 Treaty Investor Visa Application

1. **Information concerning parent company:**

a. Articles of Incorporation, seal page only

b. Financial Statement

c. Company brochure and general description of business

d. Organizational chart, number of employees and general job titles

e. Corporate ownership of parent company; documents substantiating each tier of ownership, i.e., trusts or holding companies. Stock registers and the first page of the organizational documents of each entity generally suffice. Copies of passports for each shareholder.

2. *Information concerning the U.S. company or enterprise:*

   a. Articles of Incorporation, first page only

   b. Financial Statement

   c. Description of business, business plan, Pro Forma financial

   d. U.S. organizational chart

   e. Lease or proof of ownership of U.S. premises

   f. Job descriptions

   g. Amount of capital invested in U.S. business; documents evidencing transfer of funds from Canadian parent company to U.S. subsidiary and application of funds.

   h. Proof of ownership of U.S. company, i.e. stock register

3. *Information concerning the Alien:*

   a. Personal data: name, date and place of birth, address in foreign company

   b. Resumé detailing employment history and salaries

   c. Educational history

   d. Details regarding accompanying family members, if any

H-1 Professional Visa Application

1. *Information concerning the employee:*

   a. University degree(s)

   b. Complete resumé with date and place of birth, home address abroad, address in the U.S., list of prior employers with your job description at each place

156

of employment.

c. Your salary with U.S. employer

2. *Information about the U.S. employer:*

a. Articles of Incorporation for the U.S. employer

b. Gross and net annual income of the U.S. employer; if company is a start-up, send a Pro Forma.

c. Brochure, if any, for U.S. employer or its corporate group.

L-1 (Intracompany Transferees in an Executive, Managerial or Specialized Knowledge Capacity) Visa Application

1. *Information concerning the parent company:*

a. Articles of Incorporation

b. Financial Statement

c. Company brochure and general description of business

d. Organizational chart, number of employees and general job titles

e. Corporate ownership of parent company; documents substantiating each tier of ownership, i.e., trusts or holding companies. Stock registers and the first page of the organizational documents of each entity generally suffice. Copies of passports for each shareholder.

2. *Information concerning the U.S. company or enterprise:*

a. Articles of Incorporation and organizational documents

b. Pro Forma financial statement

c. Description of business

d. Proposed U.S. organizational chart

e. Lease or proof of ownership of U.S. premises

f. Applicant's job description

g. Amount of capital invested in U.S. business; documents evidencing transfer of funds from parent company to U.S. subsidiary.

h. Proof of ownership of U.S. company, i.e., stock register

i. Federal tax identification number

3. *Information concerning the Alien:*

a. Personal data: name, date and place of birth, address in foreign company

b. Resumé detailing employment history and salaries for most recent position and last residence addresses

c. Educational history

d. Details regarding accompanying family members, if any

F. Proposed Changes In U.S. Immigration Law

The following discussion covers some of the proposed changes to the immigration laws that may affect permanent and nonimmigrant working visas. When this book was published, there was no final bill under negotiation. So this is just an advisory of some of the immigration law amendments under consideration by the U.S. Congress in early 1996.

Permanent Residence Employment-Based Visa Categories

The specific categories will be unchanged. The total number of permanent residence visas may be reduced from the current number of 140,000 to 75,000. The INS issued approximately 123,000 employment-based green cards in 1994. The reduction may cause quota waits for unskilled workers but should not effect multinational managers.

Labor Certification

There is a proposal to eliminate labor certification for immigrant workers and replace labor certification with a fee paid to the Department of Labor. The fee would equal 20 to 30% of the first year salary.

L-1A

The new law may require L-1 international organizations to have a minimum of 20 employees in the U.S. and 100 employees world-wide. This minimum employee requirement is not likely to pass because it eliminates small business in general and Canadian businesses in particular.

H-1B

Companies may be divided into "dependent" and "nondependent" classes. Dependent means that over 15%

of the work force has H-1B visas. In such a case, the employer must provide training programs for U.S. workers and pay more than the prevailing wage. There are several variations on this idea. At this time, it's impossible to tell what version, if any, will pass.

There are also proposals to reduce H and L visa validity to three years, and to require between three and five years experience outside of the U.S. for H-1B professional workers.

E-2 Eligibility

There is a proposal to require a minimum investment of $250,000.

Family Class Green Card

Expect to see the brother-sister category eliminated. Green cards for adult children will be restricted or eliminated. Green cards for elderly parents may be conditioned upon the sponsor guaranteeing medical coverage and support. The reduction of family class categories will force more people to apply for employment-based categories. This may result in quota waits for all employment-based visa categories.

Investor Category

There is a proposal to eliminate the $500,000 investment level.

Other Possible Changes

Extraordinary Ability, National Interests, Researchers and Scholar categories all face elimination or restrictions.

Author's Predictions

I predict the following changes will occur:

- Elimination of brother-sister categories.

- Requirement of experience for H-1B professional workers, and training requirements for dependent employers.

- Reduction in the number of employment-based visas to approximately 100,000 per year.

- All sponsors for family-class green card petitions must guarantee support and medical insurance.

About the Author

Henry Liebman is a 44-year-old attorney living and practicing law in Seattle, Washington. After serving as a tax specialist for Touche Ross and Company, Mr. Liebman became an associate for Franklin and Watkins Attorneys at Law. He then joined Franco, Asia, Bensussen. Mr. Liebman is now managing partner in Coe, Nordwall & Liebman, Attorneys at Law. Mr. Liebman travels extensively to Asia in conjunction with his legal practice. Mr. Liebman has three children, Nathaniel, Rachel and Catherine, and his recreational pursuits include golf, hiking, mountain-climbing and world-wide travel.

Legal Assistance

There are many law firms able to help with your immigration needs. The author's Seattle-based firm, Coe, Nordwall and Liebman, was first established in 1904, and provides legal services to an international clientele. One of the founders, Albert M. Franco, who has practiced law since 1940, led the U.S. Army G-2 in Kobe, Japan, immediately following World War II, and served as a consultant to the U.S. Agency for International Development in Central and Latin Americas. Two members of the firm have served as Legislative Assistants to the U.S. House of Representatives. Firm partner and author, Henry G. Liebman, concentrates on international legal matters and manages the firm's international and immigration law practice. He is the Business Immigration Ombudsman for PACE, a tri-lateral trade council for owners and managers of small- and mid-sized companies in Canada, the U.S., and Mexico.

Main Office:

Coe, Nordwall & Liebman
Attorneys at Law
720 Olive Way, Suite 1300
Seattle, WA 98101-1812
Telephone: (206) 624-5622
FAX: (206) 625-9218

Coe, Nordwall & Liebman may also be contacted overseas through:

Liaison Offices:

Japan

C/O U.S.A. Information Center
Attn: Junko Nishikiori
Telephone: 813 3408 2258
FAX: 813 3408 3814

Taipei

Magness Group
Attn: Charles Wang
FAX: 886-2-776-3665